PHILIP ALLAN
LITERATURE GUIDE
FOR GCSE

PHILIP ALLAN

LITERATURE GUIDE

FOR GCSE

OF MICE & MEN

JOHN STEINBECK

Steve Eddy

PHILIP ALLAN
UPDATES

With thanks to Jeanette Weatherall for reviewing the manuscript of this book.

Philip Allan Updates, an imprint of Hodder Education, an Hachette UK company, Market Place, Deddington, Oxfordshire OX15 0SE

Orders

Bookpoint Ltd, 130 Milton Park, Abingdon, Oxfordshire OX14 4SB
tel: 01235 827827
fax: 01235 400401
e-mail: education@bookpoint.co.uk
Lines are open 9.00 a.m.–5.00 p.m., Monday to Saturday, with a 24-hour message answering service. You can also order through the Philip Allan Updates website: www.philipallan.co.uk

© Philip Allan Updates 2010
ISBN 978-1-4441-0872-9
First printed 2010

Impression number 7
Year 2015 2014

Printed in Spain

Hachette UK's policy is to use papers that are natural, renewable and recyclable products and made from wood grown in sustainable forests. The logging and manufacturing processes are expected to conform to the environmental regulations of the country of origin.

Contents

Getting the most from this book and website

How to use this guide

You may find it useful to read sections of this guide when you need them, rather than reading it from start to finish. For example, you could decide to read the *Plot and structure* section in conjunction with the novel or the *Context* section before you start reading the novel. The sections relating to assessments will be especially useful in the weeks leading up to the exam.

The following features have been used throughout this guide:

● **What are the main events of the novel?**

Target your thinking

A list of **introductory questions** to target your thinking is provided at the beginning of each chapter. Look back at these once you have read the chapter and check you have understood each of them before you move on.

Build critical skills

Broaden your thinking about the text by answering the questions in the **Pause for thought** boxes. They are intended to encourage you to consider your own opinions in order to develop your skills of criticism and analysis.

Pause for thought

Grade-boosting advice

Pay particular attention to the **Grade booster** boxes. Students with a firm grasp of these ideas are likely to be aiming for the top grades.

Grade *booster*

PHILIP ALLAN LITERATURE GUIDE **FOR GCSE**

Key quotations are highlighted for you, and you may wish to use these as evidence in your examination answers.

Key quotation

'Guys like us, that work on ranches, are the loneliest guys in the world.'

Be exam-ready

The **Grade focus** sections explain how you may be assessed and distinguish between higher and foundation responses.

Grade *focus*

Get the top grades

Use the **Text focus** boxes to practise evaluating the text in detail and looking for evidence to support your understanding.

Text **focus**

Develop evaluation skills

Review your learning

Use the **Review your learning** sections to test your knowledge after you have read each chapter. Answers to the questions are provided in the final section of the guide.

Test your knowledge

 Don't forget to go online for even more free revision activities and self-tests: **www.philipallan.co.uk/literatureguidesonline**

Introduction

How to approach the text

A novel is, above all, a narrative. A large part of the storyteller's art is to make you want to find out what happens next, and therefore to keep you reading to the end. In order to study *Of Mice and Men* and to enjoy it, you need to keep a close track of the events that take place in it. This guide will help you to do that, but you may also benefit from keeping your own notes on the main events and who is involved in them.

However, any novel consists of much more than its events. You need to know the story well to get a good grade in the exam, but if you spend a lot of time simply retelling the story you will not get a high mark. You also need to keep track of a number of other features.

First, you need to take notice of the setting of the novel — where the events take place — and how this influences the story. You also need to get to know the characters and how Steinbeck lets us know what they are like. Notice what they say and do, and what other people say about them. Think about why they behave in the way they do — their motives — and what clues the author gives us about this.

As you read on, you will notice themes: the ideas explored by the author in the book. You may find it easier to think about these while not actually reading the book, especially if you discuss them with other people. You should try to become aware of the style of the novel, especially on a second reading. This means how the author tells the story.

All these aspects of the novel are dealt with in this guide. However, you should always try to notice them for yourself. This guide is no substitute for a careful and thoughtful reading of the text.

Page references

Page references are given for the New Longman annotated edition of the text (ISBN 978-0-582-46146-8) and for the New Longman plain edition (ISBN 978-0-582-82764-6) prescribed by AQA. For example, a reference to A101, P76 means that a quotation appears on page 101 of the annotated edition and page 76 of the plain edition.

Context

- **What is 'context'?**
- **How did Steinbeck's life influence his work?**
- **How did the Depression, bad farming and the weather help to create the poverty that is the background to the novel?**
- **What part is played by the 'American Dream' in the novel?**
- **How racist and sexist was California in the 1930s?**
- **What was life like on a ranch?**
- **How is the novel socially relevant to modern Britain?**

The 'context' of a novel means the combined social, historical and literary factors that influenced what the author wrote. All exam boards except CCEA treat *Of Mice and Men* as an 'other cultures' text, so it is important to be aware of how it reflects American society in the 1930s. The novel focuses on a relatively poor and deprived class of men on whom the US economy depended. It is set in California in the early to mid-1930s, during a period known as the Depression (or the Great Depression). The novel was published in 1937.

Key locations in the novel — the story is set near the town of Soledad

John Steinbeck

Steinbeck was born in 1902 in Salinas, near the coast of California, 160 km south of San Francisco and 40 km north of Soledad, the town featured in *Of Mice and Men*. His father managed a flour mill, owned an agricultural store which went bankrupt, then worked for Spreckels Sugar before becoming County Treasurer. Steinbeck Senior (whose first name was also John) passed on a love of nature to his son — which reveals itself in the opening of *Of Mice and Men*. Steinbeck's mother was a former school teacher who encouraged a love of fiction in her son and helped him to become a fluent reader by the age of five.

At high school Steinbeck wrote short stories, reading them to friends and sending them to magazines. He went to Stanford University in 1919 but was never an outstanding student. Although he attended classes for six years, he never completed his degree. However, he did continue his writing and met other writers who encouraged him in his work.

TopFoto

John Steinbeck

Perhaps a more important influence in Steinbeck's early life was his work as a labourer, during university vacations and in a two-year break from his studies. He worked digging canals, then on farms and in packing plants and a sugar-beet factory. On leaving Stanford in 1925 he went to New York and became first a construction worker, then a reporter. During his time as a travelling labourer in California he worked on ranches like the one in *Of Mice and Men*, witnessing an event on which he later based a key scene in this novel. When the novel was published, he told a *New York Times* reporter:

I was a bindlestiff [a travelling working man whose belongings are contained in a rolled up bindle, or bundle] myself for quite a spell. I worked in the same country that the story is laid in. The characters are composites to a certain extent. Lennie was a real person. He's in an insane asylum in California right now. I worked alongside him for many weeks. He didn't kill a girl. He killed a ranch foreman. Got sore because the boss had fired his pal and stuck a pitchfork right through his stomach. I hate to tell you how many times. I saw him do it. We couldn't stop him until it was too late.

(Quoted in J. Parini, *John Steinbeck: A Biography*, Henry Holt, 1995)

Although he was concerned about the plight of the working man, Steinbeck avoided becoming an explicitly political writer. His aim, based on his own experience, was to promote understanding in a non-judgemental way. In a 1938 journal entry he wrote:

> In every bit of honest writing in the world there is a base theme. Try to understand men. If you understand each other you will be kind to each other. Knowing a man well never leads to hate and nearly always leads to love.

> **Grade *booster***
>
> Be aware of Steinbeck's non-judgemental approach to social issues, reflected in the completely neutral original title of *Of Mice and Men*: 'Something that Happened'.

Steinbeck married his first wife, Carol Henning, in 1930. They lived in Pacific Grove, which inspired Steinbeck's first really successful novel, *Tortilla Flat* (1935). The sale of the film rights relieved the Steinbecks from financial worries. Steinbeck's next book, *In Dubious Battle*, the story of workers caught in the power struggle between union bosses and employers, was a controversial bestseller. By the time he wrote *Of Mice and Men* he was financially secure. However, his journal reveals that he still suffered agonies of doubt about his ability as a writer.

> **Pause for thought**
>
> Once you have read *Of Mice and Men*, ask yourself how far Steinbeck remains true to his aim of trying to understand men (and women) when it comes to this novel. For example, compare his treatment of Crooks with that of Curley. Does he help us to understand both men equally?

Steinbeck's first marriage broke down in 1941 and he married Gwyndolyn Conger, with whom he had two sons. In 1948 he was devastated when his close friend Ed Ricketts died in an accident. He divorced again in the same year. In 1950 he married Elaine Anderson Scott, with whom he remained until his death in 1968.

The Depression

The Depression began with the Wall Street Crash in 1929, when the New York Stock Exchange collapsed. In other words, the value of shares in companies traded on the exchange fell dramatically. Investors struggled to sell their shares while they were still worth something, and this made share prices fall even lower. As a result, businesses went bankrupt and fortunes were lost overnight. People became wary of investing in business, so there was widespread unemployment and poverty.

Bad farming leads to the Dust Bowl

In America, the problem was made worse by bad farming practices and drought. In once-fertile Oklahoma, over-farming and low rainfall meant that the topsoil became eroded and exhausted, creating the Dust Bowl.

TopFoto

A farm in the Oklahoma Dust Bowl

Thousands of poor farm workers, including owners of now worthless land, headed west to California. Unskilled, uneducated workers like the novel's main characters George and Lennie were at the mercy of the bosses. Men were considered lucky to find any work. On ranches like the one in *Of Mice and Men*, wages were low and conditions squalid. Steinbeck made himself unpopular with employers by writing socially critical books like *Of Mice and Men*, but, if anything, real-life conditions were worse than those he described.

The 'American Dream'

When people began to emigrate from Europe to America, most had hopes and dreams for their success in this new land. America did not have the same rigid class system as there had been in England and Europe, and there was a lot of land. Up until about 1920, there was still land waiting to be claimed and farmed. America became the land where — in theory — anyone who worked hard could 'make good' and become rich and successful. In reality, it was not that easy.

George and Lennie are, arguably, believers in the 'American Dream'. How far George really believes in it you will have to judge, but at the point just before Lennie does one 'bad thing' too many, both men, together with Candy, seem to believe they really can save enough money to buy some land and live free, happy lives, growing their own food and being self-sufficient.

Curley's wife has her own version of the 'American Dream'. In the 1930s, the film industry, based even then in Hollywood, was growing. This was before television, and even in small towns people flocked to the cinema to escape the harsh reality of everyday life. Some, like Curley's wife, dreamed of becoming stars of the screen themselves. As with the land-owning dream of George and Lennie, in theory it could happen, but in reality it was unlikely.

Ann Ronan Picture Library/HIP/TopFoto

Curley's wife aspires to be a film actress like Greta Garbo, pictured here

Pause for thought

George and Lennie do not want to get rich: they just want to be able to settle down on their own smallholding. Do you think Steinbeck wants us to feel that even this modest ambition is too much for them to hope for?

Racism

Steinbeck, himself part-Irish, part-German, has been criticised for not representing the ethnic diversity of the Californian ranch workers. Yet there is at least one member of an ethnic minority — Crooks, an embittered black man half-crippled from being kicked in the back by a horse. Until 1865, slavery was still legal in the USA. In fact, the economy of the Southern states, such as Mississippi, Alabama and Georgia, depended heavily on slave labour, especially for the production of cotton. The Civil War was fought partly over slavery: Northerners wanted it banned, so the South tried to leave the Union. The Northern victory in 1865 freed the slaves, but black people were still regarded as second-class citizens.

In *Of Mice and Men*, Crooks has some social contact with the other ranch workers but he is not regarded as an equal. This is driven home dramatically when Curley's wife tells him 'I could get you strung up on a tree so easy it ain't even funny' (A113, P88–89). This is when he attempts to assert his right to privacy. Her comment, and his passive reaction to it, shows that he really has no rights.

Poor black workers on a farm

The position of women

Only one woman appears in *Of Mice and Men* — Curley's wife. Lennie's Aunt Clara is mentioned but does not appear in person. The women who run the local brothels are also described.

Text focus

Look carefully at Section 3 from 'Whit said, "If you got idears, you ought ta come in town with us guys tomorra night"' to '"Well, a guy got to have some fun sometime," said Whit' (A78–80, P56–58). Read it several times.

- Whit is not a major character, but in this scene he speaks in a lively, forthright and unguarded way that is in contrast to George's careful reticence. Whit describes the local brothel, giving an alternative view of women to the one we see in Steinbeck's presentation of Curley's wife. Whit admires and quotes Susy's sense of humour, and, ironically, the fact that she 'never talks dirty'. He also appreciates her relaxed manner: 'If a guy don't want a flop [sex], why he can just set in the chairs.' Essentially, he tells George that the place is clean, comfortable, good fun, good value and well-run.

- This is a positive though obviously limited view of women. It seems that Whit and the other ranch men are comfortable with Susy and her 'girls'. By contrast, they are uncomfortable with Curley's wife. This is partly because of the risk of angering Curley, but also because, in a sense, they have double standards when it comes to women.

The fact that Curley's wife is never given a name is significant. It shows that in the male world of the ranch her identity is seen only in terms of her husband. It is almost as if he owns her. She is an interesting and controversial character.

Pause for thought

As you read the novel, think about how far Curley's wife is to blame for her situation, and how fairly you think Steinbeck portrays her.

Steinbeck does not portray Curley's wife as someone worthy of much respect. She is a pathetic character who relieves her boredom by flirting with the ranch workers, who generally try to ignore her so that they do not get into trouble with Curley. Nevertheless, you should bear in mind that women, especially uneducated women, in rural California in the 1930s had few opportunities and were seldom regarded by men as equals. They were expected to be conventionally feminine, or motherly (like Lennie's Aunt Clara), or were treated as commodities whose sexual favours could be paid for in a brothel. They were not expected to have careers or to be taken seriously.

Grade booster

Try to develop your own views on characters, and to collect evidence to back these views up. Considering whether Curley's wife is an innocent victim or gets what she deserves is an example of this.

Life on the ranch

Life on the ranch is tough, although the boss is better than some. He gives his men whisky at Christmas. He is said to take his anger out on Crooks, the black stable buck, at times, but at least he keeps him on at the ranch.

The living conditions on such ranches were extremely basic, if not squalid. When George is shown his bed he worries, justifiably, that it may contain lice ('pants rabbits').

Steinbeck himself worked on a ranch for a while and the ranch portrayed in the novel is probably typical of Californian ranches at the time. Some of the workers had permanent jobs but many were itinerant workers who moved about the country from one ranch to another pursuing work. George and Lennie are able to get work on the ranch in the novel because it is harvest time.

There is a pecking order on the ranch — a hierarchy of status. It is clear that the boss is at the top of the hierarchy, while Slim, the mule driver, is not far beneath him. Highly skilled workers like Slim were permanently employed on ranches and did not usually have to go looking for work. Crooks, on the other hand — another permanent worker — is at the bottom of the hierarchy. Curley's wife, who is low down on the scale and is in a sense oppressed by Curley, is still able to threaten Crooks.

Workers outside a ranch house

Comparison with modern times

Although you will not directly earn marks in a GCSE exam for being able to compare the social context of *Of Mice and Men* with modern times, it may help you to understand the novel more fully. For example, comparisons have been made between the Californian ranch workers of the 1930s and immigrant workers in modern Britain, such as the Chinese cockle pickers who died in Morecambe Bay in 2004, or Eastern European immigrants. Since many of these workers are immigrants from developing countries, working illegally in Britain, they are not protected by British employment law. In California in the 1930s, few laws protected agricultural labourers and there was a plentiful supply of workers because unemployment was high. As a result, they could easily be exploited. This kind of social injustice is a major theme in *Of Mice and Men*. One could also compare the 1930s Depression with the world recession that began in 2008.

Review your learning

(Answers are given on p. 84.)

1 How did the Depression create unemployment?
2 How did the Dust Bowl in Oklahoma help to keep wages low in California?
3 Why was the 'American Dream' possible in America but not in Britain or Europe?
4 What is Curley's wife's dream?
5 From what you know so far, does the novel seem relevant socially to modern Britain?

 More interactive questions and answers online.

Plot and structure

- What are the main events of the novel?
- How do these events unfold, section by section?
- How does Steinbeck create a structure in these events?
- How and why is this novel like a play?

Steinbeck does not call the separate parts of the novel 'sections', and he does not number them or give them titles. For convenience in this guide they are referred to as sections and numbered.

Plot

Section 1

- A peaceful scene by a river is described.
- George and Lennie are on their way to new jobs.
- George makes Lennie give up a dead mouse.
- George tells Lennie how to behave at the new ranch.
- George complains about Lennie, then regrets this.
- They eat a supper of tinned beans.
- Lennie persuades George to tell him again about their dream of owning land.
- George tells Lennie to come back to this place if he gets into trouble.

Steinbeck begins *Of Mice and Men* by carefully 'painting' a scene. The place he describes is idyllic — it is like a little paradise. We hear of the Salinas River, which has 'slipped twinkling over the yellow sands in the sunlight' (A18, P1), and of the animals that come there. We also hear of boys and tramps who visit the pool. There is a sense of peace and natural harmony.

Steinbeck introduces his two main characters into this scene in a very cinematic way. We hear their footsteps, then see them emerging into the space by the pool. We receive our first clues about their relationship here. Lennie walks behind George and almost knocks him over when George stops. George's first words are a warning to Lennie not to drink too much water and make himself ill.

Steinbeck uses this section to tell us about the two main characters and their relationship, and to explain their situation. We discover that George is small, intelligent and careful and looks after Lennie, who is big and well-meaning but slow-witted and childlike. They have come to take jobs, but were dropped off far from the ranch by a lazy bus driver and have had a long walk on a hot afternoon. This reminds us that men in their position are likely to be poorly treated.

Steinbeck uses a clever but simple device to reveal from the two men's conversation that they have come to take up work on a ranch: Lennie has a poor memory and has already forgotten where they are going, so George has to tell him. We also learn why the men left their previous jobs when George warns Lennie about his behaviour on the new ranch: 'An' you ain't gonna do no bad things like you done in Weed, neither' (A24, P7). This — and the incident of George taking a dead mouse away from Lennie, who likes to stroke mice but kills them accidentally — foreshadows what happens later in the novel.

Section 2

- The bunk house is described.
- Candy shows George and Lennie where they will sleep.
- George and Lennie meet the boss, then Curley.
- George warns Lennie to avoid Curley.
- Curley's wife is introduced and George warns Lennie against her.
- George and Lennie meet Slim and Carlson.
- Candy has an old dog, and Slim's dog has puppies.

Like the first section, this one begins with a setting — the bunk house. Steinbeck's description of it reflects its simple and functional character. The men's shelves for personal belongings consist of apple boxes nailed to the wall. The floor is unpainted.

This section also introduces most of the other characters. Steinbeck has already made sure that we will identify primarily with George and Lennie by introducing them in Section 1. We now tend to see the other characters from their point of view.

Candy, the old swamper who cleans the ranch buildings, shows George and Lennie the bunk house. George sees a can of insecticide and is worried that their beds will contain 'pants rabbits' — lice (A39, P20). Candy is anxious to reassure them. We have a preview of the boss when Candy mentions twice how angry the boss was when the two new men failed to turn up the previous evening, and how he took out his anger on Crooks. In this way, Steinbeck gives us a preview of Crooks too. He is a 'nice fella' who 'reads a lot' (A41, P22).

The two men's meeting with the boss is of dramatic interest. First, George has to explain why they have arrived late. The boss accepts the

explanation but is suspicious of George not letting Lennie answer for himself. He also wants to know why they left their job in Weed. Again, he accepts George's explanation.

We catch a glimpse of Candy's old dog, who is now no use for anything, and smells.

Curley enters, looking for his wife because he is a jealous and suspicious husband. George takes an instant dislike to this aggressive and unpleasant little man and warns Lennie to keep away from him.

Candy now plays a minor role on the ranch, but he is an important character in the novel. He previews other characters, telling George and Lennie about them before they appear in person. He tells them about Curley's wife, whom he calls 'a tart' (A50, P31). When she appears at the bunk house door looking for Curley, George already knows he should be wary of her. When she leaves, he warns Lennie 'fiercely' to keep away from her (A54, P35).

Slim, the skinner (mule driver), speaks to George and Lennie kindly and with interest, but without prying. His entry is followed by that of Carlson, who jokes about Lennie's size and name (Lennie *Small*) (A57, P38). Carlson suggests to Slim that he should get Candy to shoot his old dog and replace it with one of Slim's pups.

The section ends with another brief, jerky appearance from Curley, still looking for his wife. He looks George over as if measuring him up. George's dislike for him intensifies.

Section 3

- George confides in Slim.
- Lennie has been given a pup.
- Carlson persuades Candy that his dog should be shot.
- George, Lennie and Candy plan to buy land.
- Curley attacks Lennie and gets his hand crushed.

The section begins in the evening, after work. Outside there is still sunlight, but inside it is shadowy. George thanks Slim for giving Lennie a pup. Slim comments on George and Lennie travelling together, overcomes George's defensiveness, and hears how George came to feel responsible for Lennie. George knew Lennie's Aunt Clara, who had taken in Lennie as a baby. When she died, Lennie just came along with George when he went to work and they got used to each other. George confesses that he 'used to have a hell of a lot of fun' with Lennie, playing jokes on him and looking clever by comparison with him (A66, P44). Then one day he told Lennie to jump into the river and Lennie nearly drowned, but he still thanked George for rescuing him. This cured George of playing jokes on Lennie.

We learn why George and Lennie had to leave Weed. Lennie frightened a girl by touching her dress and fearfully clinging onto it when she 'lets out a squawk' (A67, P45). The girl claimed she had been raped and the two men had to hide in a ditch to escape a lynching party. Slim acknowledges that Lennie 'ain't mean', adding that he can 'tell a mean guy a mile off' (A68, P46). We see Lennie's childlike nature in his delight at the pup, which he tries to smuggle into the bunk house.

Carlson enters from a game of horseshoes, commenting on how good Crooks is at the game. It is interesting that we hear this about Crooks yet have still not met him in person. Carlson once again complains that Candy's old dog is of no use to anyone, or even to himself. Candy defends the dog, saying that he used to be a good sheepdog, and George tries to change the subject for Candy's sake. Carlson will not be put off. He insists that the dog should die.

The subject is suspended temporarily when Whit enters and shows Slim a letter in a Western magazine. It is a fan mail letter to one of the magazine's story writers. It appears to have been written by a man who recently worked at the ranch — a fact that impresses Whit. This underlines the sad lives of ranch workers, impressed by cowboy stories and the minor achievement of appearing in print in a cheap magazine.

There follows a moment of dramatic intensity after Carlson finally persuades Candy to let him shoot his dog. Carlson leads the dog out. The men's awkward attempts to make conversation repeatedly fall into silence, until finally a shot announces that the dog is dead

Pause for thought

We hear more about Crooks in this section. What effect do you think Steinbeck hopes to achieve by telling us about characters, through other characters, before we meet them in person?

Text focus

Look carefully at Section 3 from 'Slim said loudly, "One of my lead mules got a bad hoof"' to 'Then he rolled slowly over and faced the wall and lay silent' (A75–76, P53–54). Read it several times. This extract generates tension by slowing the pace right down. For a whole page nothing much happens, yet the tension is acute and the silence is almost an extra, invisible character. Slim tries to counter the silence by speaking loudly. Look at how often Steinbeck mentions silence:

- 'It was silent outside. Carlson's footsteps died away. The silence came into the room. And the silence lasted.'
- 'The silence fell on the room again. It came out of the night and invaded the room.'

- 'and the little snapping noise drew the eyes of all the men in the room [it breaks the silence]'
- 'The silence fell on the room again. A minute passed, and another minute.'
- 'There came a little gnawing sound from under the floor [which is a momentary relief]'
- 'The silence was in the room again. A shot sounded in the distance.'

The silence is personified — described as if it is a person. Notice how it sounds threatening: 'It came out of the night and invaded the room.' Someone reading this extract for the first time will not know it, but Steinbeck emphasises this moment because the shooting of Candy's dog foreshadows the shooting of Lennie at the end of the novel.

Crooks finally appears, telling Slim that Lennie is handling the pups too much. Shortly after this, the talk turns to the subject of women. Whit speaks admiringly of Curley's wife. George at first refuses to be drawn on the subject. However, when Whit talks about how she can't leave 'the guys' alone, and adds that 'Curley's pants is just crawlin' with ants' (he is uncomfortably jealous about his new wife) (A78, P56), George speaks out. Warning of events to come later in the novel, he declares: 'She's gonna make a mess. They's gonna be a bad mess about her' (A78, P56).

George's comment leads Whit to invite George on a trip to a brothel in town on Saturday night. He speaks appreciatively of 'Susy's place'. George says he might come but does not want to pay for sex as he and Lennie are trying to save some money.

Lennie asks George how long it will be before they can save enough money to buy their smallholding and 'live on the fatta the lan' (the goodness of the land) (A83, P61). Lennie persuades George to tell him again how their life will be, and especially about the rabbits that Lennie will get to look after. Candy listens with quiet attention. Finally, he asks if the two men know a farm they can buy cheaply. George is defensive, but when Candy asks if he can buy into the scheme with the $300 he has saved together with the $50 he will be owed, they begin to believe that their dream could come true.

The scene changes abruptly when Slim enters the bunk house, scowling and followed by Curley. We see Slim's high status in the fact that Curley, normally full of himself, is trying to placate Slim. Evidently, Slim is sick of Curley jealously suspecting him of having designs on his wife. Curley insists 'I didn't mean nothing, Slim. I just ast [asked] you' (A89, P67).

Pause for thought

Lennie asks George why it is that a 'face' playing card (Jack, Queen or King) is the same either way up (A82, P60). Since Steinbeck tends to include details for a purpose, why do you think he mentions this? Is it a symbol? If so, of what?

The men show their contempt for Curley. Carlson insultingly accuses him of letting his wife 'hang around bunk houses' (A90, P68). In response, Curley threatens Carlson, who laughs, calls Curley a 'punk', and threatens to kick his head off. Even old Candy joins in, taunting Curley about his 'Glove fulla Vaseline' (Curley is said to be keeping one hand soft to fondle his new wife). Smarting with these insults, Curley looks for someone he can safely attack and picks on Lennie, who Curley mistakenly thinks is laughing at him.

Curley brutally attacks Lennie, who merely tries to cover his face and 'bleats' with terror (A91, P69). When George finally tells Lennie to 'get' Curley, Lennie catches hold of the little man's fist and crushes it. Slim tells Curley he had better say that he got his hand caught in a machine, or else he will have to face the embarrassment of people knowing the truth.

Section 4

- Crooks's room is described.
- Lennie visits Crooks in his room.
- Crooks makes Lennie think that George might leave him.
- Candy joins Lennie and Crooks. They talk about the 'dream' farm.
- Curley's wife comes in. Crooks tries to make her leave and she threatens him.

Like other sections, this one begins with a description of a scene. This time, the scene is the room occupied by Crooks, the stable buck. His job is a relatively permanent one, so he has his own room and can have his personal possessions spread around it, although we are told that the room 'was swept and fairly neat' (A99, P74). We learn a lot about Crooks. The fact that his room is full of the tools of his trade, and harnesses for the horses and mules, suggests that work takes up most of his life.

Crooks is rubbing 'liniment' (medicinal lotion) into his painful back when Lennie appears. The other men have gone into town and Lennie is probably lonely without George. The embittered Crooks is far from friendly. However, perhaps because he is secretly lonely, he is eventually defeated by 'Lennie's disarming smile' (A101, P76) and lets him stay.

Crooks reveals that he is not 'a southern negro' (A102, P77), suggesting that he feels himself to be a cut above black people with a more recent family history of slavery. It then occurs to Crooks to torment Lennie by suggesting that George might never come back. He tells Lennie that he would be taken to 'the booby hatch' (an insane asylum) and tied up 'like a dog' (A104, P79). For a moment, Crooks, who normally has no power or

status beyond being good at playing horseshoes, enjoys exercising some power over Lennie and picturing him in a more powerless situation than his own.

Pause for thought ⏸

Crooks is embittered, lonely and the only black man on the ranch, in an area where there are very few black people. His life seems grim. Do you think there is anything he could do to improve it?

Lennie starts to think that someone really has hurt George, and Crooks has to reassure him to ensure his own safety. Relaxing again, Crooks drifts into memories of his own childhood. The mention of 'alfalfa' (a crop grown to be fed to animals) leads Lennie to talk about the 'dream farm' and his rabbits again, which in turn leads Crooks to pour scorn on the dream and on all hopes for the future. He bitterly sums up his view: 'Nobody never gets to heaven, and nobody gets no land. It's just in their head' (A106, P81).

The next person to enter is Candy. Crooks is no more friendly to him than he was at first to Lennie, although he says irritably 'You can come in if you want' (A107, P82). Candy is unsure: 'I do' [don't] know. 'Course, if ya want me to.' Crooks speaks 'brutally' to the two white men about their dream (A108, P83). But then, amazingly, he changes his mind and offers to come and work for them in return for his keep.

It is at this moment of hope that the mood changes again, when Curley's wife appears. She comments that, while she gets on well with any one man on his own, when two men are together they will not speak to her because each man is afraid that the other will 'get something' on them (A110, P85) — that is, be able to claim that he was flirting with Curley's wife.

Key quotation

Curley's wife calls Crooks, Lennie and Candy 'a bunch of bindle stiffs — a nigger an' a dum-dum and a lousy ol' sheep' (A111, P86). 'Bindle stiffs' are homeless workers who carry all their possessions in a bindle (bundle).

When the men refuse to tell her the truth about how Curley's hand was crushed, she becomes angry and indignant, complaining bitterly that she has such poor company on a Saturday night.

When she tries to flirt with Lennie, Crooks defends him by trying to order her out of his room. She responds by threatening to have him lynched, and he quickly becomes passive and obedient.

When Curley's wife finally leaves, George returns and Lennie is safe again, for now. Crooks's moment of hope has passed, thanks to Curley's wife. He now pretends he was just joking about joining the 'dream farm'. Alone in his room again, he returns to what he was doing before Lennie came along — applying liniment to his back.

Section 5

- The barn is described.
- Lennie has killed his puppy.
- Curley's wife tells Lennie her life story.

- Lennie unintentionally kills Curley's wife.
- Lennie goes to the pool by the river.
- Curley's wife's body is found.
- The men set off to hunt for Lennie.

It is Sunday afternoon, so the men are playing horseshoes. Steinbeck describes the barn, then focuses on Lennie, who is sitting sadly with his puppy, which he has accidentally killed. He gets angry with the pup for dying. Just then, Curley's wife enters the barn and comes to talk to him. She tells him she is lonely.

Lennie tries not to talk to Curley's wife, but her bitterness at the way everyone tries to avoid her spills over and she tells Lennie her life story. This is largely about how she could have joined a travelling show or become a film star in Hollywood. A man told her he was 'in pitchers' (in the movie business) (A124, P96) and promised to write to her from Hollywood and send for her. She thinks her mother stole the letter.

TopFoto

Curley's wife confides to Lennie that she dislikes Curley (2003 stage adaptation)

Lennie tells Curley's wife about the 'dream farm' and his fondness for rabbits. She seems to have some sympathy for Lennie. Knowing how Lennie likes to stroke soft things, she makes the mistake of inviting him to stroke her hair. He strokes too hard, and she gets angry. She jerks her head away and Lennie clutches her hair. She screams and he covers her mouth so that she will not get him into trouble. Soon, he has broken her neck. Realising that he has done 'another bad thing', he sneaks out to go and hide by the pool by the river, as George has told him to do if he gets into trouble.

Candy is the first to find the body. Horrified, he fetches George, who for a short time anxiously considers what to do. He thinks at first that Lennie will just be locked up, perhaps even treated well. Then he realises that Curley will want him dead. He asks Candy to wait a short time, then go and tell the others about the death while he goes somewhere else, so that it will not seem as if he was involved. George then takes this opportunity to take Carlson's Luger (a pistol). Left alone with the body in the barn, Candy vents his anger and disappointment at Curley's wife for ruining his 'dream farm' plans with George and Lennie.

When the men see the body, Curley predictably wants to kill Lennie. No one seems to wonder if it could have been an accident, although Slim seems reluctant to track Lennie down and suggests that perhaps Curley should stay with his wife. Carlson finds that his Luger has gone, so it is assumed that Lennie has taken it, although this would be completely out of character. Lennie is now regarded as armed and dangerous. George's weak suggestion that the gun could simply be lost is ignored, but he is at least able to send the search party off in the wrong direction while he goes to find Lennie.

The section ends with a despairing Candy lying down in the hay and covering his eyes.

Section 6

- The quiet scene at the pool by the river is described.
- Lennie sits and imagines himself being told off.
- George tells Lennie about the 'dream farm' for one last time.
- George shoots Lennie.

The final section of the book begins, like the others, with a description of a scene. This time, however, we have returned to the opening scene beside the Salinas River. The story has turned full circle, coming back to where it started. We even see the water snake and heron from Section 1, but this time the heron catches the snake. In a small way, this seems to foreshadow what is about to happen.

Lennie sits by the river. He tries to reassure himself by telling himself that he has done the right thing in following George's instructions to come to this place if he ever got into trouble. However, he is then beset by what appear to be hallucinations or paranoid fantasies. First, he sees his Aunt Clara, who berates him for how selfishly he has treated George when George has always done so much for him. Then she is replaced by a giant rabbit that taunts Lennie, calling him a 'crazy bastard' (A142, P111) and saying that George is going to leave him.

Lennie is shouting at the rabbit when George appears. He humours Lennie by going through the motions of complaining about what an easy life he is sacrificing by being with Lennie. Then, prompted by Lennie, he tells his friend one last time about how they have each other, how they are going to get a farm, and how Lennie will 'get to tend the rabbits' (A146, P115).

While Lennie giggles with happiness, George paints a picture of heaven on earth. He reassures Lennie that he is not angry with him and never has been. As the voices of the men from the ranch approach, George tells Lennie that they are going to make their dream come true 'right now'. Then George shoots Lennie in the back of the head.

A numbed George lets Carlson believe that he took the gun from Lennie and shot him in self-defence. As the novel closes, Slim, who unlike Carlson realises what has happened, reassures George that he had no choice. Slim leads George back towards the ranch. Carlson is left completely uncomprehending. He cannot think what could possibly be bothering George and Slim.

> **Key quotation**
>
> George: 'Ever'body gonna be nice to you. Ain't gonna be no more trouble. Nobody gonna hurt nobody nor steal from 'em.' (A147, P116)

> **Key quotation**
>
> 'Now what the hell ya suppose is eatin' [bothering] them two guys?' (A149, P118)

Structure

Whereas the plot of the novel is its sequence of events — what happens — the structure of the book means the shape that these events take or the pattern they form. We may not be aware of structure as we read, but the structure of a well-written novel can contribute to our sense of satisfaction and fulfilment in reading it.

'Neither a novel nor a play'

The structure of *Of Mice and Men* is strongly influenced by the fact that Steinbeck wrote it deliberately as a cross between a novel and a play. He told his agents in 1936:

> The work I am doing now is neither a novel nor a play but it is a kind of playable novel. Written in novel form but so scened and set that it can be played as it stands.

Although Steinbeck intended *Of Mice and Men* to be published as a novel, he anticipated adapting it for the theatre, which he later did. Therefore,

each section could be regarded as a scene in a play. Each section has a single setting and we are made aware of the time of day. It is also easy to keep track of the overall time frame:

- Section 1   The pool by the Salinas River (Thursday evening).
- Section 2   The bunk house (Friday morning).
- Section 3   The bunk house (Friday evening).
- Section 4   Crooks's room (Saturday night).
- Section 5   The barn (Sunday afternoon).
- Section 6   The pool by the Salinas River (Sunday, late afternoon to early evening).

You will notice that the action is spread over only three days. In plays, the action often takes place over a short period of time because this makes it easier to build up and sustain dramatic momentum, and there is no need to find a device to let the audience know that a long period of time has passed.

The fact that each section has a single setting also makes it easy to stage. In some novels, the action flits from one setting to another. A character could be in bed, in the kitchen, on the street, on a train — all in the space of a few minutes. This kind of action would be difficult to show on stage. In *Of Mice and Men*, each section or scene is easy to show on stage. The indoor scenes — in the bunk house, Crooks's room and the barn — are easiest to show, but even the scenes by the river would not be hard to suggest with lighting and sound effects.

You will also notice how each section begins with a description of the scene (the pool, the bunk house, Crooks's room). This gives Steinbeck an opportunity for detailed descriptive writing. However, it also provides 'stage directions' to tell anyone producing the novel as a play exactly how each scene should look.

Another dramatic feature is the fact that, after the two main characters have been introduced in the first section, each subsequent section focuses on at least one major piece of action:

- Section 1   We meet George and Lennie. We find out about their relationship and why they are here.
- Section 2   George and Lennie meet two threats — first Curley, then his wife.
- Section 3   Carlson shoots Candy's dog. Lennie crushes Curley's hand.
- Section 4   Curley's wife confronts Crooks, Candy and Lennie.
- Section 5   Lennie kills Curley's wife.
- Section 6   George kills Lennie.

Grade *booster*

See the 'big picture'. The structure of this novel is cyclical: it begins and ends at the pool by the Salinas River. In Section 1 the pool is a place of harmony; in Section 6 it is shown in a darker and even sinister way. The novel begins with the two men's dream of happiness; it ends with Lennie still essentially innocent and George still poor and landless. However, in a sense, Lennie has entered the 'promised land' of the dream, with the help of George's suggestion and his own faith.

The narrowed focus — on a single event — in the last three sections helps to speed up the action.

The way we get to know the characters is also dramatic. Apart from George, Lennie and Candy, we find out something about important characters even before they appear in person. Candy tells George and Lennie (and therefore us) about the boss, Curley, Curley's wife and Crooks. The boss gives a brief description of Slim. This helps to fix them in our minds, which is useful in a play, where the audience needs to grasp quickly who everyone is.

In most plays the action tends to progress from a position of conflict and tension to one of resolution — in order for the audience to go away feeling satisfied. The main source of tension in *Of Mice and Men* is Curley's wife and her unhappy relationship with Curley. A different kind of tension exists between dreams and harsh reality. Both kinds of tension contribute to the death of Curley's wife.

Review your learning

(Answers are given on p. 84.)

1 What does George complain about after he and Lennie have quenched their thirst at the pool?

2 Which two people does George warn Lennie to stay away from in Section 2?

3 When (times and days of the week) does the novel start and end?

4 What do you think would be lost if the novel were staged as a play?

5 Would it be a better novel if George and Lennie escaped at the end?

More interactive questions and answers online.

Characterisation

- What is each character like?
- What does each character want?
- What are the relationships between characters?
- How does Steinbeck reveal the characters to us?
- What evidence can we find to help us assess each character?

Lennie Small

Lennie is, in a sense, the central character, although you could argue that it is his relationship with George that Steinbeck focuses on. The events of the novel revolve around Lennie and he is the main tragic figure, despite the fact that Curley's wife also dies, and at his hands. However, Lennie's lack of intelligence and initiative make him an unlikely tragic hero.

Lennie Small is big and strong, but has well below average intelligence (1992 film adaptation)

Lennie's relationship with George

We learn that Lennie has attached himself to George after Lennie's Aunt Clara died. He is big and strong, but of well below average intelligence. He trusts George completely — a fact made painfully obvious to George when, as he relates to Slim, he once told Lennie to jump into a river for a joke. Lennie nearly drowned.

Lennie is happy to follow George's lead in everything. We see this immediately by the way he still walks behind George, even in the open, almost knocking George over when he stops suddenly. Lennie is anxious to please George and trusts in his ability to do what is best for them both. He hates it when George is angry with him, as occurs in Section 1 when George bitterly complains about Lennie's behaviour getting them into trouble in Weed. Lennie does not need to say he is upset. George has only to look at Lennie's 'anguished face' to know. Lennie tries to appease George by creeping close to him and telling him that if they had any ketchup he would let George have it all. It is his way of trying to make a personal sacrifice for George's sake.

A 'nice fella'

Other characters in the novel comment on Lennie's good nature. Slim says of him: 'He's a nice fella. Guy don't need no sense to be a nice fella. Seems to me sometimes it jus' works the other way around' (A66, P44). Curley's wife, too, tells Lennie: 'You're nuts. But you're a kinda nice fella. Jus' like a big baby' (A126, P98). Even the cynical and isolated Crooks is won over by 'Lennie's disarming smile' (A101, P76). In fact, the only person on the ranch who dislikes Lennie is Curley, and that is because Curley resents 'big guys' because he is small and has an inferiority complex. Despite this, Lennie has no desire to hurt Curley when Curley attacks him in Section 3. He is frightened and pleads with George to make Curley stop. The only reason he grabs hold of Curley's hand and crushes it is because George tells him to 'get 'im'.

Cunning

Lennie, despite being trusting and unintelligent, can be surprisingly sneaky at times — though with little success because George knows him so well. The first time we see this is in Section 1, when Lennie retrieves the dead mouse that George has thrown away: 'What mouse, George? I ain't got no mouse' (A26, P9). Even when George threatens to 'sock' him, Lennie keeps up the pretence for a moment longer before pleading to be allowed to keep it.

Lennie behaves in a similar way when he tries to smuggle his puppy into the bunk house, and when he later tries to conceal the fact that he has killed the puppy.

Another aspect of Lennie's character that seems to contradict the image of him as the trusting fool is that he has an animal instinct for danger.

Pause for thought

For Lennie's death to be seen as tragic, we need to identify with him. Do you feel Steinbeck makes it possible for you to identify with Lennie — despite his lack of intelligence — and therefore to feel sympathy for him? If so, what factors help you to do this?

Key quotation

Slim (speaking of Lennie): 'He's a nice fella.' (A66, P44)

Curley's wife (to Lennie): 'You're nuts. But you're a kinda nice fella. Jus' like a big baby.' (A126, P98)

As early as Section 2, he suddenly bursts out with 'I don' like this place, George. This ain't no good place. I wanna get outta here' (A55, P36).

The 'dream farm'

Lennie, more than anyone in the novel, believes in the dream of owning land and being self-sufficient. He is especially excited about being allowed to tend the rabbits and feed them alfalfa. It is a sad moment when, near the end of the novel, he has a hallucination in which a giant rabbit tells him he is not fit to tend rabbits. However, this moment gives way to his final vision of the dream farm, which allows him to die happy.

George Milton

Other characters are puzzled by George's travelling with Lennie, whose unintelligence makes him poor company and a dangerous liability. The boss suspiciously demands of George 'Say — what you sellin'? I said what stake you got in this guy? You takin' his pay away from him?' (A43, P24). Slim is more open-minded but still comments, 'Funny how you an' him string along together' (A65, P43). Even George seems puzzled at times about why he stays with Lennie.

George is intelligent

The fact that George stays with Lennie says a great deal about George's character. George is, after all, an intelligent man. He has enough vision to dream of an ideal future for himself and Lennie. He has practical foresight, telling Lennie to come and hide by the pool if he ever gets into trouble, and spotting immediately that Curley and his wife could cause trouble. He also shows quick-wittedness. For example, when he learns that Lennie has killed Curley's wife, he realises that people might think he had something to do with it. He therefore asks Candy to let him go to the bunk house while Candy breaks the news, so that the men will assume George was in the bunk house all the time. But this also gives him a chance to steal Carlson's gun. Even at such a difficult time he is already planning ahead to the moment when he will have to shoot Lennie.

George is modest

George is modest about himself. When Slim calls him 'a smart little guy', he replies that if he were clever he would not be doing a poorly paid manual job on a ranch: 'buckin barley for my fifty and found [fifty dollars a week, plus board and lodging]' (A65, P43). The real reasons for George doing this kind of work are more complicated. Although Steinbeck tells us nothing about George's background, there is nothing to make us think

Key *quotation*

George (to Lennie): 'When I think of the swell time I could have without you, I go nuts. I never get no peace.' (A30, P13)

that he has had the advantages of family, wealth or education. It would be difficult for George to pursue a career, or even hold down a job in one place for long, while he is committed to looking after Lennie.

George is careful and clean-living

It is part of George's character to be careful. This shows in a number of ways. In Section 1, he tries to prevent Lennie from drinking 'scummy' water that might be dirty and make Lennie ill (A20, P3). He is angry when he thinks that the previous occupant of his bunk may have had lice (A39, P20). He is cautious when it comes to telling others about the dream he shares with Lennie. When Candy overhears George and Lennie discussing it and asks if they know where to buy a farm, George is 'on guard immediately' and will not tell him where the farm is. He gradually opens up, but still watches Candy 'suspiciously' (A86, P64).

George is also careful with money. When Whit invites him to visit the brothel in Soledad, he responds cautiously: 'Might go in and look the joint over' (A79, P57). A little later, he explains that he and Lennie are 'rollin' up a stake' (saving money to buy their farm). He adds that he 'might go in an' set and have a shot [sit and drink a glass of whisky]' (A80, P58) but he will not pay two and a half dollars for a prostitute.

> ### Pause for thought
>
> What do you think is George's attitude towards sex? When Candy tells him that Curley keeps his glove full of vaseline to keep his hand soft for fondling his wife, he seems quietly disgusted: 'That's a dirty thing to tell around' (A49, P30). He also has no time for Curley's wife herself, saying as little as possible to her. He has no interest in visiting prostitutes with the other men. On the other hand, he says that if he did not have to look after Lennie, he could 'maybe have a girl' (A24, P7). Is George morally upright or rather puritanical?

George's morality

Although the action of the novel is spread over only a few days, Steinbeck reveals that George has the capacity for moral growth. George confides in Slim that he used to enjoy feeling clever compared with Lennie, and he used to have fun at Lennie's expense until Lennie's near-drowning made him stop. This suggests that George has the humility to see when he has done wrong and is prepared to change. The compassion he has learned to feel for Lennie is part of why he stays with him.

Why George stays with Lennie

George complains that he could have an easy time without Lennie. However, you might ask yourself if he stays with Lennie purely out of a sense of moral duty. Although he says that Lennie is 'dumb as hell' (A65, P43), he is proud of Lennie's ability to work hard and take orders: 'Jus' tell Lennie what to do an' he'll do it if it don't take no figuring' (A64–65, P42–43). He also points out to people that Lennie is neither 'crazy' nor

> ### Grade *booster*
>
> Note 'foreshadowing'. Steinbeck prepares us for George's mercy killing of Lennie by Candy's comment in Section 3: 'I ought to of shot that dog myself, George. I shouldn't ought to of let no stranger shoot my dog' (A89, P67). George does not let a stranger shoot Lennie.

'mean'. When George tells Lennie about their dream, an important part of it is that they are not like other migrant workers, because they have each other — they are not lonely.

George reveals most about his reasons for staying with Lennie in his conversation with Slim at the start of Section 3. George explains 'I ain't got no people' — he has no family (A67, P45). He says that men who travel alone 'don't have no fun' and eventually 'get mean'. Note how this contrasts with George's complaints to Lennie about what a 'swell time' he could have without Lennie. He tells Slim, 'you get used to goin' around with a guy an' you can't get rid of him' (A67, P45).

Despite George's occasional complaints, it seems that his relationship with Lennie is mutually rewarding

On the whole, it seems that, despite George's occasional complaints, his relationship with Lennie is mutually rewarding: they both benefit from it. It is enormously difficult for George when, at the end of the novel, he has to shoot Lennie rather than let him be caught and either lynched or put into an asylum. This is his ultimate act of taking responsibility for his friend.

Candy

Candy is an elderly man who has a permanent job on the ranch as a swamper — keeping the bunkhouse clean. He is introduced as 'a tall, stoop-shouldered old man' (A38, P19). His stooping body language suggests hopelessness as well as age. He has lost his hand in an accident on the ranch, which is why his job is permanent. This, together with the fact that Candy received some compensation, shows that Steinbeck is being fair to ranch owners, not just portraying them as selfish exploiters. However, the fact that Candy lost his hand at all suggests that health and safety standards were poor.

Candy is, on the whole, good-natured. He speaks well of Crooks and of the boss, revealing that the boss treated his workers to a keg of whisky at Christmas. He calls Crooks a 'nice fella' (A41, P22) and the boss a 'pretty nice fella' (A41, P22). He shows some ability as a judge of character in his comments on Curley, observing that Curley picks fights with 'big guys' because he resents the fact that they're bigger than him (A48, P29). He also shows a sense of injustice when he says that when Curley beats a 'big guy', 'Ever'body says what a game guy Curley is' (A48, P29) and when he loses, people say that the 'big guy' should pick on someone his own size.

Candy is also a gossip. For example, he tells George about Curley keeping one hand 'soft for his wife' (A49, P30).

One important detail to remember about Candy is that he has a smelly old dog. Candy proudly recalls what a good sheepdog he was. However, both Candy and the dog are now old and not much use to anyone. The insensitive Carlson badgers Candy to shoot the dog, and Candy eventually gives in and lets Carlson do it.

Lennie, George and Candy

Despite his age and infirmity, Candy is still able to have hopes. When he overhears George and Lennie discussing their 'dream farm', Candy jumps on this idea as his salvation. When Curley's wife dies, and he reluctantly accepts that this means the end of the dream, he is bitterly disappointed. She is the one character for whom he has shown dislike, calling her 'a tart' (A50, P31). When she is dead, he feels only anger towards her: 'gradually his sorrow and his anger grew into words. "You God damn tramp," he said viciously' (A132, P104).

The boss

The boss is 'a little stocky man' who wears jeans like a working man but also 'high-heeled boots and spurs to prove he was not a laboring man' (A41, P22). Steinbeck spends relatively little time on him, and never names him. Yet the boss is in one sense an important character, in that he owns and runs the ranch, hires and fires workers, and determines their pay and conditions. He also has importance in a dramatic sense in that he allows his son Curley to behave as he does, even though it interferes with the smooth running of the ranch.

Grade *booster*

Candy's gossipy nature, though believable, is also a narrative device by which Steinbeck can quickly reveal information about the characters — especially important in a stage version of the novel. Thus Candy is like the 'Chorus' in ancient Greek plays, and in some Shakespeare plays, such as *Henry V*.

Pause for thought

We last see Candy lying down in the hay, covering his face with his arm in despair at the end of Section 5. Is your sympathy for him lessened by his lack of sympathy for Curley's wife?

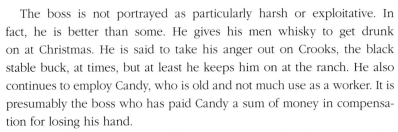
The boss is not portrayed as particularly harsh or exploitative. In fact, he is better than some. He gives his men whisky to get drunk on at Christmas. He is said to take his anger out on Crooks, the black stable buck, at times, but at least he keeps him on at the ranch. He also continues to employ Candy, who is old and not much use as a worker. It is presumably the boss who has paid Candy a sum of money in compensation for losing his hand.

The boss suspects George of exploiting Lennie, but this suggests that he has a sense of justice.

Curley

Curley, the boss's son, has little to recommend him. He is aggressive and yet cowardly — Carlson calls him 'yella as a frog belly' (A90, P68) — mean-minded, vengeful and jealous. The best we can say about him is that he might have been a nicer man had he been a bigger one: he has an inferiority complex because of his size.

He makes the most of being the boss's son, ordering George and Lennie around. However, he is cowed by Slim's status and afraid of Carlson, which is why he picks on Lennie, who he thinks will be an easy target. When Lennie crushes Curley's hand, Curley could have Lennie 'canned' (fired). However, Slim knows Curley well enough to prevent this, telling Curley, 'I think you got your han' caught in a machine' (A92, P70). If Curley tells anyone it was Lennie, Slim will make sure that Curley becomes a laughing stock.

Candy says that Curley keeps one hand in a glove full of vaseline in order to keep it soft for his wife. If this is true, it suggests that Curley likes to think of himself as a good lover. However, he does not seem to be loving towards his wife. They have been married for only a short time, yet he leaves her alone on the ranch on a Saturday night to visit a brothel with the ranch hands. He is jealously suspicious that she might take an interest in other men. When she dies, his reaction is not grief at losing her but anger and a desire for revenge: 'He worked himself into a fury. "I'm gonna get him. I'm going for my shotgun. I'll kill the big son-of-a-bitch myself"' (A133, P105). He seems to see his wife as a possession that has been stolen from him.

Curley's wife

Her identity

The first thing you may notice about Curley's wife is that she is never called anything else. Unlike the other main characters, she is never given a proper name. There is some room for your personal interpretation here. However, Steinbeck probably wants to show that the ranch hands never see her as a real person with an identity of her own. Rather, they see her as something belonging to Curley. This is partly because they do not want to risk their jobs by being friendly to her and upsetting Curley.

Ironically, we never actually see Curley and his wife together except when she is dead. They make occasional appearances looking for each other, but they never find each other. Curley's jealous suspicion makes him look for her, and she probably looks for him out of boredom. This is one of the things that makes her a somewhat pathetic figure.

'A tart'?

If you answer an exam question about Curley's wife, you should think about how Steinbeck wants us to see her. To what extent should we believe in what other characters say about her? Before we meet her in person, we hear about her from Candy. He tells George that he has seen her 'give Slim the eye' (look lustfully at him), and that she is 'a tart' (A49–50, P30–31).

When we meet Curley's wife in person, Steinbeck reinforces the negative image created by Candy. It seems a bad sign that her first appearance blocks out the light: 'the rectangle of sunshine in the doorway was cut off. A girl was standing there looking in' (A53, P34). Her physical appearance also reinforces Candy's view: 'She had full, rouged lips and wide-spaced eyes, heavily made up. Her fingernails were red. Her hair hung in little rolled clusters, like sausages.' Even her 'nasal, brittle' voice makes her seem unpleasant. Her body language seems sexually provocative: 'She put her hands behind her back and leaned against the door frame so that her body was thrown forward.' However, Lennie's gaze makes her feel uncomfortable, so any sexuality in her body language may be unconscious.

George condemns her as soon as she leaves the bunk house: 'Jesus, what a tramp' (A54, P35). Whit appreciates her looks: 'Well, ain't she a looloo?' (A78, P56) but still criticises her for not hiding her sexuality ('She ain't concealin' nothing') and for looking at the men ('She got the eye goin' all the time on everybody'). The only person who is pleasant to her is Slim, and even he focuses on her looks: 'Hi, Good-lookin'' (A54, P35).

The worst of Curley's wife

We see the worst of Curley's wife when she is bored and lonely on a Saturday night and visits Crooks's room. As usual, she says she's looking for Curley, and as usual she is 'heavily made up' (A109, P84). At first, she smiles at the men — Crooks, Lennie and Candy — but when she fails to get a friendly response she comments, 'They left all the weak ones here.' Then she comments, perceptively, that when the men are together they are afraid to be friendly to her, each worried that the other will 'get something' on him (have something to threaten him with — telling Curley).

We see the misery of her marriage when she complains bitterly about Curley, who only seems interested in what he is going to do to all the people he dislikes. She is pleased that his hand has been crushed, and she admires Lennie for doing it. However, she is unsympathetic to the three men, clearly using them only to relieve her boredom. She 'contemptuously' calls them 'a bunch of bindle stiffs [homeless men carrying all their possessions in a bundle] — a nigger an' a dum-dum and a lousy ol' sheep' (A111, P86). But she is also indignant that they refuse to tell her what really happened to Curley's hand.

Key quotation

'I could get you strung up on a tree so easy it ain't even funny.'
(A113, P88–89)

MGM/The Kobal Collection

When Curley's wife makes the mistake of letting Lennie stroke her hair, it is probably out of a mixture of sympathy and vanity

Although it is easy to feel some sympathy with Curley's wife in this scene, it becomes harder when she threatens to get Crooks lynched. She is voicing the racism of the time, but she is also asserting herself over the one person who is clearly below her in the ranch pecking order, and whom she can therefore threaten without fear of consequences, giving herself some slight sense of power and status.

The best of Curley's wife

Grade booster

Don't fall into the trap of dismissing Curley's wife in the way that the ranch hands do. It is important to be aware of her social context as a lone woman in 1930s California.

Steinbeck's portrayal of Curley's wife is at its most sympathetic just before she dies, in the scene in the barn with Lennie. We see that her dreams are even more hopeless than those of George and Lennie. As she hinted in the earlier scene in Crooks's room, she has dreams of becoming famous. First, she was prevented by her mother from joining a travelling show. Then she met a man who promised to put her 'in the movies' in Hollywood (A124, P96). Pathetically, she believes her mother must have stolen the man's letter, since he promised to write. This is why she has settled for marrying Curley.

The disappointment that Curley's wife confides in Lennie, and the slight sympathy she shows him, makes it easier for us to sympathise with her. She tells Lennie: 'You're nuts. But you're a kinda nice fella. Jus' like a big baby. But a person can see kinda what you mean' (A126, P98). When she makes the fatal mistake of letting him stroke her hair, it is probably out of a mixture of sympathy and vanity.

> **Key quotation**
>
> **Curley's wife: 'I coulda made somethin' of myself…Maybe I will yet.'**
> **(A124, P96)**

Slim

Slim plays an important role on the ranch and in the novel. He is a mule skinner — someone who drives the mules that pull carts, ploughs and other machinery on the ranch. Steinbeck presents him as evidence that noble qualities can be found in the humble working man. Whereas Curley has no virtues, Slim has no faults.

> **Text focus**
>
> Slim is first shown combing his 'long, black, damp [just washed] hair straight back' (A55, P36), showing that he is clean and well groomed. Steinbeck's description of him is almost too full of praise: 'he moved with a majesty only achieved by royalty and master craftsmen…the prince of the ranch…capable of killing a fly on the wheeler's butt with a bull whip without touching the mule.'
>
> Slim has a natural authority and an 'understanding beyond thought'. His hands are 'as delicate in their action as those of a temple dancer' (A56, P37). This is a surprising simile (an image comparing two things), given that Slim is a ranch worker. It helps to create a certain air of mystery about him, like his lean and ruggedly handsome ('hatchet') face that disguises his age: 'He might have been thirty-five or fifty.'
>
> Above all, Slim is to be respected. When he speaks, a hush falls on the room. Even when he stands up, he does so 'slowly and with dignity' (A58, P39).

Pause for thought

What is your view of Slim? Is he too good to be true? Would he have more depth as a character if Steinbeck had given him a few faults?

Slim shows tact and understanding when he speaks to George, and he somehow draws George out of himself without pressing him, so that George confides in him. He is similarly quick to understand and sympathise at the end of the novel, when George has to shoot Lennie. Steinbeck describes Slim as looking 'kindly' and speaking 'gently' (A56, P37). He is generous too, giving Lennie one of his pups and telling George 'No need to thank me about that' (A64, P42).

Despite being gentle and sensitive, Slim is also tough. When Curley annoys him by repeatedly asking about his wife, Slim is described as 'scowling', and he speaks angrily to Curley despite Curley being the boss's son: 'If you can't look after your own God damn wife, what you expect me to do about it? You lay offa me' (A89–90, P67–68). When Curley attacks Lennie, Slim is about to go to Lennie's defence until George stops him. After the attack, it is Slim who makes sure that Lennie will not get into trouble for crushing Curley's hand. It is also Slim who makes the important point that you don't have to be intelligent to be a 'nice fella'.

Crooks

Crooks is the stable buck — he looks after the horses and mules. He is introduced when Candy mentions to George that the boss takes his anger out on Crooks because he is black, explaining: 'Ya see the stable buck's a nigger' (A40, P21). In the routinely racist world of California in the 1930s, this passes for an explanation. For the men on the ranch, Crooks's colour is his defining feature. However, Candy does add that Crooks is a 'nice fella' and that he 'got a crooked back where a horse kicked him' (A41, P22). We also learn that he has a talent for the game of 'horseshoes', which the men play as a pastime.

Crooks is the focus of the fourth section in the novel. Steinbeck devotes one of his scene-setting section openings to Crooks's room. In the process, he tells us a lot about Crooks and his life. He has a room of his own because he is a relatively permanent skilled worker on the ranch, and because, being black, he is not allowed in the bunk house. Having his own room means he can have his possessions spread about it. Most of them relate to his work, such as a harness and leather-working tools. He does have a few personal possessions, although some of these also appear to be work-related: 'several pairs of shoes, a pair of rubber boots, a big alarm clock and a single-barrelled shotgun' (A98, P73). His books and magazines, however, have nothing to do with work. They mark him out as an intelligent and literate man. His copy of the 'California civil code' suggests that he has an interest in justice even if he is unlikely to get it. His 'few dirty books' (A99, P74) are an interesting detail. It is unclear whether they are pornographic or just grubby.

Crooks keeps his room neat and clean, 'for Crooks was a proud, aloof man' (A99, P74). Steinbeck also tells us 'He kept his distance and demanded that other people keep theirs.' Crooks seems proud that he is not 'a southern negro' with a recent family history of slavery (A102, P77). His distance from others is accentuated by the fact that he is in pain much of the time because of his spinal injury.

His first words in the section, to Lennie, support what Steinbeck has already told us about him: 'You got no right to come in my room' (A99–100, P74–75). He scowls at Lennie, but after a while he is softened by Lennie's smile. He even seems to enjoy Lennie's company: 'A guy can talk to you an' be sure you won't go blabbin'" (A102–03, P77–78). He reveals that he is desperately lonely.

Despite apparently appreciating Lennie's company, Crooks torments him by suggesting that George might not return from town. He tells Lennie that he would be taken to 'the booby hatch' (an insane asylum) and tied up like a dog (A104, P79). He enjoys exercising this small degree of power over Lennie and picturing him in a more powerless situation than his own.

Life has taught Crooks to be cynical and pessimistic. Hence he is at first scathingly dismissive when Lennie and Candy talk about the farm they are going to buy with George. However, it is as if he has to be like this to avoid the risk of raising his own hopes:

> Crooks interrupted brutally. 'You guys is just kiddin' yourself. You'll talk about it a hell of a lot, but you won't get no land…I seen too many guys with land in their head. They never get none under their hand.' (A108, P83)

Surprisingly, after this outburst Crooks allows himself to become hopeful. He hesitates, then offers to come and work on the farm 'for nothing — just his keep' (A109, P84). This moment of hope is immediately soured by the appearance of Curley's wife in the doorway. None of the men wants her in the room, but when Crooks asserts his right to privacy, she threatens him. His reaction to this is dramatic (imagine how it might appear on stage):

> Crooks stared hopelessly at her, and then he sat down on his bunk and drew into himself…Crooks seemed to grow smaller, and he pressed himself against the wall. 'Yes, ma'am.'…Crooks had reduced himself to nothing. There was no personality, no ego — nothing to arouse either like or dislike. (A113–14, P88–89)

He is a proud man, but his survival instinct makes him become almost invisible. He puts on 'layers of protection' (A115, P90). When Curley's wife goes, we see that Crooks's hope has evaporated. He tells Candy 'You guys comin' in an' settin' made me forget. What she says is true.' The reminder of his lack of rights returns him to his lack of hope, although he is too proud to admit the truth: 'I didn' mean it. Jus' foolin'. I wouldn' want to go no place like that' (A116, P91).

Carlson

Carlson is described on his first entry as 'a powerful, big-stomached man' (A57, P38). He is fairly friendly but not very bright, as we see when he

makes the obvious joke about Lennie (whose surname is Small), 'He ain't very small,' chuckling at his own joke and repeating it.

Carlson's main role in the novel is to badger Candy into allowing his old dog to be shot. Carlson does this himself. He is insensitive to Candy's feelings about the dog, being mostly concerned about its smell. However, to be fair to Carlson, he does suggest to Slim that he should give Candy one of his puppies, and he does argue that it would be a kindness to shoot the old dog.

We also see Carlson as a tough man who is not afraid of Curley. He calls him a 'God damn punk…yella as a frog belly' and threatens to kick his head off (A90, P68). However, we see his unintelligence and insensitivity again at the end of the novel. He wrongly assumes that it is Lennie who has taken his Luger pistol. After George has shot Lennie, Carlson ends the book with the uncomprehending question, 'Now what the hell ya suppose is eatin' [bothering] them two guys?' (A149, P118). He fails to understand that George, and even Slim, could be upset by Lennie's death.

Grade *booster*

Carlson is given a realistic mixture of good and bad features. How do you think this compares with the portrayals of Slim and Curley?

Grade *focus*

How will you be assessed on character-based questions?

Grades G–D

In this range of grades, candidates' answers are likely to deal with the characters as if they were real people, with little awareness of their fictional nature. There might be detailed accounts of the ranch hands' actions, and comments about them being lonely or aggressive. At this level candidates tend not to discuss the dramatic roles of the characters.

The better candidates in this range will support comments with references to the text.

Grades C–A*

In this grade range examiners will expect to see that you know about the behaviour of the characters, but also that you realise that aspects of human nature can be seen in them. The best candidates will be equally able to discuss the characters as psychologically realistic creations and as representing elements of human nature, and to comment on how they reflect American culture in the 1930s.

Use Table 1 to give yourself a clearer idea of what makes the difference between types of responses.

PHILIP ALLAN LITERATURE GUIDE **FOR GCSE**

Table 1

Character	Grade G–D	Grade C–A*
George	A clever little man who looks after Lennie even though this means he can't do what he wants.	Embodies the ideal of the noble working man, self-sacrificing and honest, co-dependent with Lennie.
Lennie	A big, strong, stupid man who likes soft things and gets into trouble a lot.	Represents animal nature (described as animal); has an instinctual awareness.
Crooks	Black cripple who likes to keep himself to himself.	'Proud and aloof man' who would like to have human contact but would rather reject it than be rejected.
Curley's wife	Vain, empty-headed woman who likes to flirt with the ranch hands and threatens Crooks with lynching.	Lonely, naive and disappointed woman; represents the situation of poor, uneducated women in 1930s America.

Review your learning

(Answers are given on p. 84.)

1 What incident made George stop playing jokes on Lennie?

2 Who do the following phrases describe?
   a 'full, rouged lips and wide-spaced eyes'
   b 'a tall, stoop-shouldered old man'
   c 'His hatchet face was ageless.'

3 Who makes the following statements and to whom? What in your opinion does each statement reveal about the speaker?
   a 'I could live so easy and maybe have a girl.'
   b 'Guy don't need no sense to be a nice fella.'
   c 'Nobody never gets to heaven, and nobody gets no land.'

More interactive questions and answers online.

Themes

- **What is a theme?**
- **What are the main themes in *Of Mice and Men*?**
- **How do these themes relate to each other?**
- **How do these themes relate to the characters?**

A theme is an idea or group of ideas that an author explores. There is no single way to define what the themes in a novel are, and in any interpretation of themes there is bound to be some overlap. Nevertheless, it is possible to reach agreement on at least the major themes in *Of Mice and Men* because it is a short novel and Steinbeck makes his intentions clear. Here is a suggested list:

- loneliness
- friendship
- shattered dreams
- injustice
- the working man

We could break these themes down into smaller sections to see how Steinbeck explores them.

Loneliness
- most ranch workers
- Candy (old, one-handed)
- Crooks (black, semi-crippled)
- Curley's wife (only woman on the ranch, in a loveless marriage)
- George: 'Guys like us, that work on ranches, are the loneliest guys in the world.' (A31–32, P14–15)

Friendship
- George and Lennie: 'We got somebody to talk to that gives a damn about us.' (A32, P15)
- Candy and his dog (shot by Carson)

Shattered dreams
- the 'American Dream' — the idea that in America everyone can succeed, and even get rich
- George and Lennie: 'we're gonna have a little house and a couple of acres an' a cow and some pigs' (A32, P15)

- Candy: 'I could of hoed in the garden and washed dishes for them guys.' (A132, P104)
- Curley's wife: 'I coulda made somethin' of myself.' (A124, P96)
- Crooks: 'Nobody never gets to heaven, and nobody gets no land.' (A106, P81)

Injustice

- working men treated badly
- racial prejudice (Crooks)
- sexual inequality (Curley's wife)
- Lennie picked on by Curley

The working man

- mistreatment
- no future
- can be noble, like Slim and George

Loneliness

In *Of Mice and Men*, Steinbeck pairs the themes of loneliness and friendship, which are almost opposites. In this novel, no one is really alone: people live and work in close proximity to each other. Yet several characters are lonely. This theme is stated clearly by George in the early pages of the book: 'Guys like us, that work on ranches, are the loneliest guys in the world' (A31–32, P14–15). He goes on to say that he and Lennie are different from other drifters because they have each other. In this way Steinbeck presents loneliness as a starting point and friendship as an escape from it.

The friendship between George and Lennie is the only one portrayed in the novel. Curley may be too unpleasant to have any friends. He certainly has none on the ranch. If characters such as Slim and the boss have friends, we never meet them. This may be partly because Steinbeck does not want to clutter the novel (or the stage) with minor characters, but it also helps to emphasise the loneliness of most characters compared with George and Lennie.

Steinbeck has given us a picture of most ranch workers as lonely, rootless souls with no friends or family connections, but the three loneliest people in the novel live permanently on the ranch. They are:

- Candy — whose best friend is his dog
- Crooks — whose colour isolates him from the other workers
- Curley's wife — who has recently married a man she neither loves nor likes

Grade *booster*

Be aware that themes interconnect: for example, friendship and loneliness; injustice and the working man. Also, an exam question may present opportunities to write about a theme, even if it is not named. A question about 'America in the 1930s' could enable you to write about shattered dreams, injustice, and the working man.

Key quotation

Ranch workers are 'the loneliest guys in the world' (A31–32, P14–15).

Grade *booster*

Exam questions may ask you to look at how Steinbeck uses a particular character to explore a theme. Learn to think about how characters are used in this way.

Examiners look for
evidence that you
engage with the
characters. It may be
hard for you to relate
to Candy, but imagine
what his life is like —
old, weak, one-handed,
no friends or family,
nothing to look forward
to. Can you forgive his
lack of sympathy for
Curley's wife?

Candy

Candy is old and has lost his hand in a farming accident. As a swamper
who cleans the living quarters, he is denied even the normal camaraderie
(comradeship) of shared work. His best friend seems to be his old dog,
which Carlson takes out and shoots. He apparently has no family he feels
he can go and live with in his old age.

Candy's loneliness is reflected in his eagerness to gossip to newcomers
George and Lennie when they arrive on the ranch, and in his ready
embrace of the dream that George shares with Lennie. He enjoys George's
fantasy of how they would just stop work and go off to a carnival or show
together if they felt like it.

Candy's loneliness is matched by his bitter disappointment when he finds
Curley's wife dead and realises that now the dream can never come true.

Crooks

We first meet Crooks properly in Section 4. Characteristically, he is alone
in his room, where he spends most of his non-working hours. Crooks is
even lonelier than Candy. As a black man, he is not allowed in the bunk
house to mix with the other workers. On the one occasion when he
was allowed in, at Christmas, he was attacked by another worker — an
incident that Candy relates with amusement to George (A41, P22).

Crooks is the only black man on the ranch and almost the only one in
the area — there is one black family in nearby Soledad. He takes pride
in not being 'a southern negro' (A102, P77). This means he has no recent
family history of slavery, but at least if he were living in the South, for
example in Alabama or Mississippi, he would have a community of black
people around him. Here in California he does not suffer the obvious
racial hatred of the South but he is very isolated. His one social outlet is
playing horseshoes with the other workers.

Crooks is a proud man and his pride makes him reject what he knows
he cannot have. Therefore, when Lennie tries to befriend him, Crooks
at first tries to send him away. He treats Candy in a similar way. Yet his
envy of Lennie's friendship with George makes him torment Lennie by
suggesting that George may never come back and that Lennie will be left
alone. Realising he can say whatever he wants to Lennie without anyone
else ever finding out, he confesses to him:

> 'S'pose you couldn't go into the bunk house and play rummy 'cause you was
> black. How'd you like that? S'pose you had to sit out here an' read books.
> Sure you could play horseshoes till it got dark, but then you got to read books.
> Books ain't no good. A guy needs somebody — to be near him.' (A105, P80)

Crooks: 'A guy goes
nuts if he ain't got
nobody.' (A105, P80).

Curley's wife

The loneliness suffered by Curley's wife is different again from that of either Candy or Crooks. She is, as far as we know, the only woman on the ranch. If the boss has a living wife, Steinbeck keeps her out of the story. For company, Curley's wife can only turn to her new husband or to other men on the ranch, but Curley is jealously suspicious if the other men give her any attention. He seems to regard her as a possession. Perhaps his own self-doubt makes him worry that she will be unfaithful.

Curley's jealous nature means that most men on the ranch try to avoid his wife for fear of losing their jobs — he is the boss's son. In addition, the men see her interest in them as improper and call her 'a tart' (A50, P31). As she puts it herself:

> 'If I catch any one man, and he's alone, I get along fine with him. But just let two of the guys get together an' you won't talk. Jus' nothing but mad...You're all scared of each other, that's what.' (A110, P85)

This means that her sole source of company is Curley, whose conversation is mean-minded and boring.

When she confides in Lennie, she again voices her dislike of Curley: 'I don't *like* Curley. He ain't a nice fella' (A125, P97). Notice the emphasis on 'like': some people marry someone they do not love, but she is newly married to a man she does not even like.

> **Key quotation**
>
> Curley's wife (on Curley): 'Spends all his time sayin' what he's gonna do to guys he don't like, and he don't like nobody.' (A110, P85)

> **Key quotation**
>
> Slim: 'Maybe ever'body in the whole damn world is scared of each other.' (A57, P38)

Friendship

It is, of course, significant that the novel's two main characters are close friends. Moreover, they have a special relationship. They are not just part of a group of friends — they are each other's only friends. Because they travel around together from job to job, it would be hard for them to make other friends. In addition, Lennie has an almost doglike devotion to George. It is unlikely that he would ever feel this for anyone else. George, for his part, despite his complaints, is devoted to Lennie.

> **Key quotation**
>
> George to Lennie: 'I could get along so easy and so nice if I didn't have you on my tail.' (A24, P7)

George speaks proudly of Lennie's strength and capacity for hard work, and he feels a responsibility towards him that gives George a purpose in the world. He explains to Slim that he used to enjoy making jokes at Lennie's expense — until Lennie nearly drowned because George told him to jump in the river. But the friendship, although unequal in a sense

because George is much more intelligent, is mutual. As George tells Slim, 'We kinda look after each other' (A57, P38). Even before this, George recites to Lennie in the words that almost spell out the theme: 'We got somebody to talk to that gives a damn about us' (A32, P15).

Lennie and George have a special relationship — they are each other's only friends (2003 stage adaptation)

Pause for thought

How far do you think George and Lennie can be said to have a real friendship, given the difference in their intelligence? Can friendship only exist between equals?

The relationship between George and Lennie is the only example of friendship in the novel — apart from Candy and his dog. In fact, Steinbeck emphasises how unusual it is by having other characters comment on it. The boss is suspicious and asks if George is taking Lennie's pay away from him. He assumes that George must be exploiting Lennie: 'I never seen one guy take so much trouble for another guy. I just like to know what your interest is' (A43, P24). Curley is similarly puzzled. When George tries to explain why he is doing the talking — 'We travel together' — Curley replies 'Oh, so it's that way', as if there were something wrong in this (A47, P28). Crooks is so envious of the friendship that he taunts Lennie, suggesting that George might never return from the brothel in town.

Slim, too, comments on the oddness of the friendship:

> 'I hardly never seen two guys travel together. You know how the hands are, they just come in and get their bunk and work a month, and then they quit and go out alone. Never seem to give a damn about nobody. It jus' seems kinda funny a cuckoo like him and a smart little guy like you travelin' together.'
> (A65, P43)

However, Slim is also the only one to comment favourably on it. He is able to see beyond the inequalities of the relationship, commenting that Lennie can be a 'nice fella' without being intelligent (A66, P44).

George finds looking after Lennie a strain at times, and of course he cannot always protect him. When Lennie makes his fatal mistake and kills Curley's wife, George can no longer save him. He can, however, make sure that he dies happy. Steinbeck has already foreshadowed this by having Carlson kill Candy's dog — his only friend — which leads Candy to confess 'I ought to of shot that dog myself, George. I shouldn't ought to of let no stranger shoot my dog' (A89, P67). George shoots Lennie in a last act of friendship and self-sacrifice, ensuring as he does so that Lennie is happily absorbed in their mutual dream of independence.

Shattered dreams

It could be argued that 'shattered dreams' is the main theme of the novel. One piece of evidence to support this is that its title is based on this theme. It comes from a line in a poem by the Scottish poet Robert Burns (1759–96). The theme of shattered dreams can be seen on several levels, outlined below.

The Garden of Eden

You may have seen the opening, before the arrival of George and Lennie, as mere scene-setting. You may even have been impatient, waiting for characters to appear and do something. But this opening does more than set a scene: it paints a picture of paradise. It shows a peaceful and harmonious natural world, the paradise in which human beings could live if they were not selfish and afraid. Section 6 returns to the same setting, but now it has lost its innocence, as shown by the heron spearing the water snake. Even Lennie's Aunt Clara and the rabbits have taken on a sinister aspect in his imagination. When George recounts their dream of a smallholding to Lennie for the final time, we know that it is now impossible. So the structure is used to reinforce this important theme.

Grade *booster*

Show awareness of the author's purpose. Steinbeck gives a clue to his purpose in the novel's title, taken from a line in Burns's poem 'To A Mouse'. Here is the line in context:

The best-laid schemes o' mice an' men
Gang aft agley [often go wrong],
An' lea'e us nought but grief an' pain,
For promised joy.

Consider how this is reflected in the novel.

Pause for thought

Some critics see the opening of the novel as portraying the Garden of Eden, as described in the book of Genesis in the Bible. Curley's wife could be compared with Eve, who gives Adam the apple that gets them both expelled from Eden. The view is given weight by the fact that Steinbeck's novel *East of Eden* uses this biblical imagery. Perhaps it is even no accident that George's surname, Milton, is the name of a famous English poet who wrote a long poem called *Paradise Lost* based on the Bible story (John Milton, 1608–74). What do you think of this interpretation of *Of Mice and Men*?

The 'American Dream'

America has been called 'the land of opportunity'. The early migrants to America went there hoping for a better life, and this tradition of hope survived. It was a land of rich material resources and space, and its society was not bound by the rigid class barriers of Britain and Europe. In theory it was possible for anyone to get rich: it was a land of equality. However, in reality there is no society in which more than a handful of people get rich. In California in the 1930s during the Depression (see the *Context* section), most people were poor and had few real opportunities. Yet opportunities that theoretically exist create expectations and disappointments. Steinbeck wanted to show the contrast between the ideal of 'the American Dream' and the reality of widespread poverty and disappointment.

Key quotation

George: 'Some day — we're gonna get the jack together and we're gonna have a little house and a couple of acres an' a cow and some pigs...' (A32, P15)

Key quotation

Crooks: 'Nobody never gets to heaven, and nobody gets no land.' (A106, P81)

'A little piece of land'

The particular version of the 'American Dream' that sustains George and Lennie is the dream of buying and farming their own smallholding and being independent. If they can manage this, they will be free from bosses, bunk houses and the need to move around from one ranch to another. The biggest attraction in this for Lennie is that they will be able to have rabbits and he will be allowed to look after them. This theme, like the other

---

Text focus

Look carefully at Section 4 from 'You're nuts' to 'They're all the time talkin' about it, but it's jus' in their head' (A106, P81). Read it several times. The bitter scorn that Crooks feels for Lennie's dream of having a farm makes him speak forcefully. Notice the harsh rhythm of his speech. The repetition of 'hunderds' (hundreds) emphasises his point. So does the abrupt comparison of 'bindles on their back' and 'same damn thing in their heads'.

Notice the power of the sentence summing up what happens to each of these hundreds of men: 'They come, an' they quit an' go on'. This is reinforced by the repeated image of 'a little piece of land in his head'.

Most powerful and damning of all is his comparison of this dream of land with the Christian dream of heaven. The double negatives are grammatically non-standard English, but here they are powerful, coupled with the repetition: 'Nobody never gets to heaven, and nobody gets no land. It's just in their head. They're all the time talkin' about it, but it's jus' in their head.'

---

main themes, is stated early in the novel. George, in response to Lennie's nagging, describes how they will have 'a little house and a couple of acres' and be free to stop work whenever they want. As Lennie puts it, they will '*live off the fatta the lan*' [the fat of the land — nature's bounty] (A32, P15).

It is only when Candy overhears the two men discussing their dream that it begins to become a real possibility, partly because he believes that it is possible, and partly because he is prepared to put his compensation money for the loss of his hand into buying the farm.

On the other hand, Crooks puts the dream into the context of harsh reality. He says he has seen hundreds of men with the same dream, and that it never comes true for any of them.

'I coulda made somethin' of myself'

Curley's wife has no interest in owning land — another reason why she is out of place on the ranch. However, she does have her own version of the 'American Dream'. She confides in Lennie shortly before he kills her that when she was 15 a travelling show came to town and one of the actors invited her to join them, but her mother said she was too young.

Then she 'met a guy, an' he was in pitchers [in the movie industry]' (A124, P96). This man promised to launch her on a Hollywood acting career and said he would write to her about it when he got back to Hollywood. She believes, rather pathetically, that her mother stole the letter (which almost certainly never came). She has married Curley because of this belief that her mother has held her back from stardom.

There is nothing to make us believe that Curley's wife really had any hope of becoming a film star. When she makes 'a small grand gesture with her arm and hand to show that she could act' (A125, P97), the effect is to make us pity rather than admire her.

> **Grade *booster***
>
> Show your awareness of American culture. Hollywood contributed to the American Dream. Audiences identified with film characters who went 'from rags to riches', and people like Curley's wife fantasised about becoming film stars themselves.

Injustice

The theme of injustice is not as strong in *Of Mice and Men* as it is in Steinbeck's longer novel *The Grapes of Wrath*. Nevertheless, it is a feature of the novel, overlapping with the themes of loneliness and shattered dreams.

There is a basic, understated sense of social injustice in the novel. There is a strong hint of this when George and Lennie make their first appearance. They have been dropped off in the wrong place by a bus

driver, so they have had a long walk. The bus driver could easily have dropped them off outside the ranch, and probably would have done so had George and Lennie not been poor migrant workers.

The story of George and Lennie having to leave Weed, where they last worked, is also an example of injustice. Lennie only wanted to touch a girl's dress, but she accused him of rape and so George and Lennie had to flee because her story would have been believed. This foreshadows the injustice at the end of the novel. Again, Lennie just wants to touch something soft and intends no harm to Curley's wife. Nonetheless, he and George would stand little chance of persuading a jury of this, let alone a lynch party led by Curley.

On the ranch, the boss is not particularly harsh or unjust but he has the power to hire and fire (remember that there were many more workers than jobs in California at this time). Most of the ranch hands shun Curley's wife because they could be fired if they upset Curley, the boss's son, by speaking to her. It is to the boss's credit that he keeps Candy and Crooks in his employment despite their injuries and reduced ability to work (especially Candy). However, bear in mind how they received their injuries in the first place. Health and safety regulations in California in the 1930s were minimal. It is likely that in a modern workplace Candy would not have lost his hand, or would have received a lot more compensation had he done so. We are told that he received $250, which amounts to about five months' pay.

Crooks is clearly a victim of injustice. As a black man, he cannot enter the bunk house. He has his own room — next to a dung heap — but he would rather have company. His lack of real rights is made clear in Section 4 when Curley's wife threatens to have him hanged if he complains about her.

However, even Curley's wife is a victim of injustice. Although she has the power to threaten Crooks because she is white, as a woman she has very little power or independence. Her attempts to find company and relieve her boredom result in the men regarding her as 'a tart'. Yet her new husband leaves her alone on a Saturday night to visit a brothel in Soledad — clearly a case of sexual double standards.

> **Pause for thought**
>
> Do you think that in some ways, Susy, who runs the brothel, is better off than Curley's wife?

The working man

All the men in the novel are working men, although the boss presumably does no manual labour (he wears high-heeled boots with spurs to prove that he does not need to) and it is unclear just how much work of any sort Curley does. George is intelligent, yet can only hope to get manual work. On this ranch he and Lennie are heaving sacks of barley. He modestly tells Slim that if he were 'bright' he wouldn't be doing this kind of work for a low wage and board.

Both George and Slim are presented as proof that the working man can be intelligent, sensitive and ethical. Slim is shown as a highly skilled worker with a remarkable wisdom and insight into life.

Steinbeck wanted to show the conditions of the working man in this novel — not so much the physical hardship, but the emotional depriva-tion of the itinerant worker travelling from ranch to ranch, lonely and ultimately without hope. The theme overlaps with the theme of loneliness, and with that of injustice, especially in relation to the injuries sustained by Candy and Crooks. However, Steinbeck does not emphasise this aspect of the working man's life.

> **Pause for thought**
>
> Steinbeck was influenced by Communist thinkers and union leaders, but was later criticised by left-wingers for not being radical enough. Do you think that *Of Mice and Men* is a socialist novel, or are its concerns more personal than political?

Grade *focus*

How will you be assessed on theme-based questions?

Grades G–D

In this range of grades, candidates' answers are likely to deal with themes purely in terms of how they relate to characters and the plot, and to see themes individually rather than as interrelated.

The better candidates in this range will support comments with references to the text.

Grades C–A*

In this grade range examiners will expect to see that you know about how the characters embody themes, and know that they do so in a variety of different ways. They will also expect you to place the themes in their cultural context. For example, disappointment could be seen as a theme that relates to Crooks, who is embittered because of the racial prejudice that he encounters. It also relates to Curley's wife, because she has dreams of stardom — her own version of 'the American Dream'.

Use Table 2 on p. 50 to give yourself a clearer idea of what makes the difference between types of responses.

Table 2

Character	Grade G–D	Grade C–A*
Loneliness	A lot of people in the novel are lonely. Crooks has to stay in his room. Curley's wife has no friends.	Many people in the novel are lonely in different ways, owing to prejudice and to mutual suspicion.
Friendship	The only friendship in the novel is between George and Lennie, although it is unequal because Lennie is stupid.	George and Lennie represent the possibility of overcoming isolation through friendship. George may be as dependent on Lennie as Lennie is on him.
Prejudice	The main example of prejudice is Crooks, whom the ranch hands look down on because he is black.	Prejudice appears in the novel in many forms. Curley is prejudiced against Lennie because of his size.

Review your learning

(Answers are given on p. 85.)

1 Which five main themes are identified in this guide?

2 Which three characters most reflect the theme of loneliness?

3 Who is especially lonely because of being 'proud [and] aloof'?

4 Who is presented as the main example of what we can call 'the noble working man'?

5 Which theme do you consider to be the most important in the novel? Think of at least three reasons for your answer.

More interactive questions and answers online.

Style

- **What features does the term 'style' refer to?**
- **How does the theatrical form of this novel influence its style?**
- **How does Steinbeck use settings?**
- **How does Steinbeck use adverbs?**
- **What use does Steinbeck make of descriptions?**
- **How realistic is the dialogue?**
- **What viewpoint does Steinbeck adopt?**
- **How does Steinbeck use imagery and symbolism?**

Anyone who has read *Of Mice and Men* will be able to retell the story more or less accurately, and you will earn no marks in the exam for doing this. Many exam questions relate to Steinbeck's characters and most candidates will be able to make some comment on them. However, an author's style is one of the less obvious features of a novel. It follows that if you write about it well in the exam, you will show the examiner that your grasp of the novel is sophisticated.

When you write about style, you are showing that you understand an important fact: the author of a novel has numerous choices. Your job as a literary critic — because that is what you are when you write your exam essay — is to identify what choices Steinbeck has made and to assess how effective they are.

The list below gives some of the main features covered by the word 'style'. Steinbeck has made choices about all of them:

- how the **settings** add to the story (e.g. the bunk house)
- how **dialogue** (conversation) is used and how realistic it is
- what **description** is included — for example, adjectives describing a character's appearance and adverbs to describe how someone speaks
- the **viewpoint** from which the story is told, especially whether it is third-person ('He went outside') or first-person ('I went outside') narrative
- **imagery** — the way in which the author uses word pictures (such as **similes** — using 'like' or 'as' — and **metaphors** — speaking about one thing as if it is something else)
- **symbolism** — e.g. the use of light to represent life and hope, and darkness (as in the bunk house) to suggest the opposite

How the theatrical form influences the style

Steinbeck wrote *Of Mice and Men* in a form somewhere between a conventional novel and a stage play. This influenced his style in several ways.

Setting and atmosphere

Apart from the opening and closing sections (or scenes), the novel is set on a ranch, and most of its characters are working men. However, you may have noticed that we never see the men working. We are never taken out into the fields to see them bucking barley. Similarly, Slim is a mule driver and Crooks looks after the mules and horses, yet we never see farm animals — apart from a brief appearance by Candy's old dog. This may in part reflect the rather closed in, restricted lives of the men. A more practical reason is that it would be hard to bring horses, mules and farm machinery on stage or to show the men moving through a field of barley.

It would be just about possible to have a dog on stage but shooting it would be impractical — and cause an outcry! Hence the dog is shot offstage. This enables Steinbeck to build up a wonderfully tense atmosphere while we wait to hear the sound of Carlson's pistol 'in the distance', telling us that he has shot the dog (A76, P54). Another example of a practical consideration for the stage used to dramatic effect is the game of horseshoes played by the men. We never actually see this. We hear about it from the men and in Steinbeck's description:

> From outside came the clang of horseshoes on the playing peg and the shouts of men, playing, encouraging, jeering. But in the barn it was quiet and humming and lazy and warm. (A120, P92)

Keeping the game outside and only overheard means that in a stage production the actors do not have to actually play it. However, both onstage and in the novel it enables Steinbeck to achieve an interesting dramatic effect. We are aware of the contrast between the two scenes: inside the barn, Lennie is grieving over his dead pup, then talking to Curley's wife, then killing her; outside, the men are enjoying their game.

Steinbeck introduces each new setting with a detailed description. This helps to set the scene, enabling us to imagine it fully. It also gives us a clear idea of the physical conditions in which the men live and provides ready-made stage directions.

The settings show the colourless and practical nature of the men's lives. In the bunk house, nothing is purely for decoration and there are no elements of luxury or comfort. The same can be said for Crooks's room in Section 4, but there the description of his tools and few personal possessions draw us into Crooks's lonely and restricted world.

Text **focus**

Look carefully at the first paragraph of Section 2, from 'The bunk house was a long, rectangular building' to 'boxes for the players to sit on' (A38, P19). Read it several times.

The description itself is detailed but plain. The detail leaves little to the imagination, while the plainness of the language reflects the dull and practical nature of the men's lives.

Steinbeck writes that 'the walls were whitewashed and the floor unpainted'. He could have written 'the walls gleamed as white as the first untrodden snow on Christmas morning, while the wooden floor was as honestly unadorned as nature intended'. The effect of this would be very different. Steinbeck departs from the plain, factual description only for a moment when he mentions 'those Western magazines ranch men love to read and scoff at and secretly believe'. This reminds us of how few recreational pursuits were open to the ranch men. It suggests they take pleasure in fantasy that enables them to escape briefly from dull and predictable lives.

Dialogue

Another theatrical feature of the novel is its use of dialogue (conversation). A stage play cannot include comments from the author: it depends on action and dialogue. All novels have dialogue, but many novels also have a lot of comment from the author on the personality traits, thoughts and feelings of the characters.

In *Of Mice and Men*, Steinbeck reveals the characters to us almost entirely by what they say and do. For example, he does not write 'Sometimes George felt frustrated and trapped by having to look after Lennie all the time.' Instead, he has George say to Lennie 'When I think of the swell time I could have without you, I go nuts. I never get no peace' (A30, P13). George's character is brought to life almost entirely through his own speech and actions.

However, Steinbeck also uses a stage technique when he has characters comment on other characters. Candy is the main character who does this, fulfilling the same role as the 'Chorus' in an ancient Greek play. For example, in talking to George he tells us about Curley, Curley's wife, the boss and Crooks before we meet them in person.

Steinbeck's dialogue is fairly realistic, because he wanted to present the lives of working men as they really were. It is not entirely realistic, because in reality people interrupt each other, talk over each other, trail off mid-sentence and make slips of the tongue. However, as we read the novel it seems realistic. This is partly achieved by Steinbeck's careful attention to the language that ranch hands used. A lot of the speech is in non-standard English. It could be called ungrammatical although, strictly speaking, it follows a non-standard grammar of its own.

One example of this is the use of double negatives. For example, Crooks declares 'Nobody never gets to heaven, and nobody gets no land' (A106, P81). The dialogue is also colloquial (familiar and informal) rather than formal, and uses a lot of slang. The word 'ain't' is usually used in place of 'is not', 'are not' or 'am not'. Colloquial phrases are used. For example, George tells the boss 'I told his old lady I'd take care of him. He got kicked in the head by a horse when he was a kid. He's awright. Just ain't bright' (A44, P25). In more formal style, this would be 'I told his mother I'd take care of him. He was kicked in the head by a horse when he was a child. He's a good man really. He just isn't very intelligent.' More obscure slang is used occasionally, as when Curley's wife calls Lennie, Candy and Crooks 'a bunch of bindle stiffs'. Steinbeck's characters also use what would, in the 1930s, have been considered quite 'bad' language at times, reflecting the reality of working men's speech.

Finally, Steinbeck attempts to reproduce the way the characters actually pronounce the words. For example, Carlson tells Curley 'you're yella as a frog belly' (A90, P68); Candy tells the dead Curley's wife 'I could of hoed in the garden' instead of 'I could have' (A132, P104) and elsewhere he says 'If he coulda used his feet' (A41, P22).

Description

Places

Steinbeck uses descriptive passages in the sections that open and close the novel, as well as including more factual 'stage directional' descriptions of the settings at the beginning of the other sections. The opening section contains some important description of the pool by the Salinas River. Significantly, it is in the present tense, hinting at a paradise that is somehow outside of time, always present. Steinbeck dwells on the description, using more words than he strictly needs to. The language appeals to the senses (especially sight and hearing) and makes the place sound calm and beautiful, in contrast to the lives of the men in the rest of the novel:

- 'The water is warm too, for it has slipped twinkling over the yellow sands in the sunlight' (A18, P1)

- 'golden foothill slopes' (A18, P1)
- 'fresh and green with every spring' (A18, P1)
- 'the leaves lie deep and so crisp that a lizard makes a great skittering if he runs among them' (A18, P1)
- 'On the sand banks the rabbits sat as quietly as little gray, sculptured stones.' (A19, P2)

People

Steinbeck also gives physical descriptions of his characters to help us picture them and to indicate something about their personalities. For example:

- George: 'The first man was small and quick, dark of face, with restless eyes and sharp, strong features. Every part of him was defined: small, strong hands, slender arms, a thin and bony nose.' (A19, P2)
- Lennie: 'a huge man, shapeless of face, with large, pale eyes, with wide, sloping shoulders; and he walked heavily, dragging his feet a little, the way a bear drags his paws. His arms did not swing at his sides, but hung loosely.' (A19, P2)

Here there is a lot of emphasis on adjectives: small, quick, dark, restless, sharp, strong, defined, slender, thin, bony. These all describe George. You might try spotting the adjectives used for Lennie in the second paragraph.

Adverbs

A noticeable feature of Steinbeck's writing style in *Of Mice and Men* is his use of adverbs to indicate the way in which a character speaks or behaves. They could be used as stage directions in a stage version of the novel but they also tell us a lot about the characters, either in general or as their moods change at particular times. The following adverbs are used, at different points in the novel, to describe the speech of George and Lennie:

- George: angrily, gently, softly, coldly, loudly, ominously, insultingly, casually, thoughtfully, wonderingly, quickly
- Lennie: gently, softly, hopefully, patiently, craftily, timidly, breathlessly, miserably, sorrowfully
- Steinbeck also uses adverbs to describe the way characters behave. For example, in the opening section:
  - 'The small man stepped nervously beside him.' (A20, P3)
  - 'George stared morosely at the water.' (A21, P4)
  - 'Lennie looked timidly over to him.' (A21, P4)

Viewpoint

The viewpoint of the novel is the position from which the author tells the story. For example, Steinbeck could have chosen to relate this story in the first person, perhaps through the eyes of George. In this case, it might begin 'I sure was angry with that bus driver. He coulda dropped us off right outside the ranch, but instead we had to walk.' Instead, Steinbeck chose to write the novel in the **third person**. This means saying 'He said', 'She did' etc. The advantage of this is that the author is not limited to describing only those things that the narrating character could know about. It also means the author can comment on characters and give us insight into them. Some authors do this at great length. However, Steinbeck hardly does it at all. One of the few examples is when he describes Crooks: 'Crooks was a proud, aloof man. He kept his distance and demanded that other people kept theirs' (A99, P74). Perhaps Steinbeck does this because other characters would probably not understand Crooks well enough to comment on him accurately. On the other hand, Crooks speaks and behaves in a way that shows he is proud and aloof, so you could argue that Steinbeck's comment is unnecessary.

Another advantage of the third-person viewpoint, but one that Steinbeck hardly uses, is the author's freedom to describe what characters are thinking or feeling. Steinbeck prefers to let their words and actions reveal this. For example, he never writes: 'Curley was furious. He desperately wanted to get his own back on Lennie.' The only exception to this self-imposed rule is when Steinbeck takes us into Lennie's distraught hallucinations at the end of the novel, beginning 'And then from out of Lennie's head there came a little fat old woman' (A141, P110).

Imagery

The term 'imagery' refers to the kind of word pictures an author creates to help us imagine what is being described. Steinbeck uses two types of image in *Of Mice and Men*:

- **simile** — when one thing is compared with another, using 'like' or 'as' (e.g. Curley 'flopping like a fish on a line' (A91, P69))
- **metaphor** — when something is described as if it actually is something else (e.g. Lennie's hand is a 'paw')

Imagery relating to nature

Steinbeck uses imagery in a relaxed and almost playful way when he describes the pool by the river in the opening section:

- 'the rabbits sat as quietly as little gray, sculptured stones' (A19, P2)
- 'A water snake slipped along on the pool, its head held up like a little periscope' (A25, P8)

However, the imagery has a hint of menace when the heron catches the water snake in the final section. This seems to suggest a fall from innocence — a realisation that death exists even in paradise. It also warns us of Lennie's death.

- 'A silent head and beak lanced down' (A140, P109)
- 'a gust drove through the tops of the trees like a wave' (A140, P109)

Imagery to describe people

Most imagery in *Of Mice and Men* is used to describe people. One noticeable feature is Steinbeck's use of images that portray characters as animals.

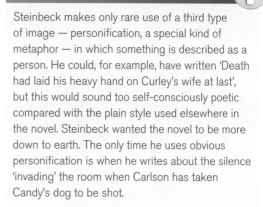

Grade *booster*

Steinbeck makes only rare use of a third type of image — personification, a special kind of metaphor — in which something is described as a person. He could, for example, have written 'Death had laid his heavy hand on Curley's wife at last', but this would sound too self-consciously poetic compared with the plain style used elsewhere in the novel. Steinbeck wanted the novel to be more down to earth. The only time he uses obvious personification is when he writes about the silence 'invading' the room when Carlson has taken Candy's dog to be shot.

Lennie

- 'he walked heavily, dragging his feet a little, the way a bear drags his paws' (A19, P2)
- 'Lennie dabbled his big paw in the water' (A20, P3)
- 'snorting into the water like a horse' (A20, P3)
- 'Lennie covered his face with his huge paws and bleated with terror' (A91, P69)
- 'his fist lost in Lennie's paw' (A92, P70)
- 'He pawed up the hay' (A128, P100)
- 'he came as silently as a creeping bear moves' (A140, P109)

Curley

- 'Curley stepped over to Lennie like a terrier' (A90, P68)
- 'The dirty little rat' (A91, P69)
- 'Curley was flopping like a fish on a line' (A91, P69)

Curley's wife

- 'her body flopped like a fish' (A128, P100)

In the case of Lennie, comparing him with a bear, a horse and a sheep ('bleated'), and referring to his hands as 'paws', suggests his animal nature.

He has the simplicity and innocence of the animal world and the strength of the bear. He also has a kind of animal instinct, which makes him tell George that he wants to leave the ranch: 'This ain't no good place. I wanna get outta here' (A55, P36). This instinct is reflected, too, in his liking for animals — rabbits, mice and his puppy. Curley is like an animal in a more negative way — a terrier because he is small and aggressive and a rat because he is vicious and underhand (according to the conventional view of rats).

Symbolism

When an author uses an image, something is compared with something else. Symbolism is related to imagery, but it is not nearly so obvious. A symbol is something that the author uses consistently to represent something else. There is rather more room for personal interpretation here: not all critics interpret a symbol in exactly the same way. Since symbols often operate at the level of the unconscious mind, even the author may not be able to give us an exact definition of what a particular symbol stands for.

To get an idea of how a symbol is open to a variety of interpretations, look at the symbolism in the opening scene of the novel. The pool by the river could be seen as:

- what might be called 'the water of life' — as whatever it is that sustains all animal and human life
- a reminder that life changes constantly and then slips away
- a peaceful pause in life's winding journey

These ideas are similar but not the same.

Steinbeck's use of light

Many critics have commented on Steinbeck's symbolic use of light. For most people, light suggests good things: mental or spiritual illumination, happiness, hope and even God. Hence the river is seen 'twinkling over the yellow sands in the sunlight' (A18, P1). As the day ends, 'the tops of the Gabilan mountains flamed with the light of the sun' (A25, P8). The mountains themselves seem to suggest hope, although it is far away. The two men build a fire and it is its light as well as its warmth that comforts and sustains them: 'as the blaze dropped from the fire the sphere of light grew smaller' (A34, P17).

The bunk house has small windows so it is gloomy inside, symbolising the lives of the ranch men. However, when Slim enters the whole place is lit up, both symbolically by his dazzling presence and literally:

Although there was evening brightness showing through the windows of the bunk house, inside it was dusk…Slim reached up over the card table and turned on the tin-shaded electric light. Instantly the table was brilliant with light, and the cone of the shade threw its brightness straight downward. (A64, P42)

Light and dark mark a contrast between the men's lives and the outside world of possibilities. The contrast can also be seen to indicate different views of the world. Thus, Slim comments on entering the bunk house: 'It's brighter'n a bitch outside. Can't hardly see nothing in here' (A56, P37). When Carlson enters the bunk house, he only comments on the darkness: 'Darker'n hell in here' (A70, P48).

In Crooks's room, the smallness of the light could be seen as symbolising the grimness and lack of hope in his life: 'a small electric globe threw a meager yellow light' (A99, P74). However, it is this light that draws Lennie to Crooks's room, so it could also symbolise human warmth or the promise of friendship. The symbolism is more obvious when Curley's wife makes her first appearance: 'the rectangle of sunshine in the doorway was cut off' (A53, P34). This seems to foreshadow (almost literally) the role Curley's wife plays in ending the hopes and dreams nurtured by George and Lennie.

Review your learning

(Answers are given on p. 85.)

1. What is the main setting of the novel?
2. Name three ways in which the theatrical form of this novel influences its style.
3. What part of speech does Steinbeck use with particular frequency, and how?
4. What does every section begin with?
5. How does Steinbeck make the dialogue realistic?

 More interactive questions and answers online.

Tackling the exam

- **How well do you need to know the text?**
- **What are tiers?**
- **How should you plan and structure your exam essay?**
- **How should you provide evidence to support your interpretation?**
- **What will turn a C essay into an A* essay?**

Knowing your text

There is no substitute for knowing the text you are studying inside out — not even reading this literature guide cover to cover! This is true whatever exam board you are studying for. If you are studying for the WJEC or CCEA specification, you will not be allowed to take a copy of the novel into the exam with you, so you will not be able to look up quotations or remind yourself of the plot. The other boards allow you to take your copy of the novel into the exam, as long as it has no handwritten notes in it. However, the time you have for writing is short, so you need to spend as little of it as possible looking up quotations and reminding yourself of the text.

Even if you are not allowed to take the text into the exam, you will be given a passage to read on which your first question, at least, will be based. Be sure to make the most of this passage, including commenting on its style if that is relevant to the question. However, make sure you also write about the rest of the novel if asked to do so.

Although you will get no marks for simply retelling the story, it is important to know it well so that you can refer to it correctly and find your way round it quickly if you need to look something up. You should have a sound grasp of the following:

- the main events
- the sequence in which they occur
- the part played by each character in the main events

It is helpful, though not essential, to be able to refer confidently to the sections. For example, 'Section 4 focuses on Crooks.' You should also be able to spell the names of all the characters and know their position on the ranch. The examiner will not be impressed if you write that 'Curly is the

PHILIP ALLAN LITERATURE GUIDE **FOR GCSE**

boss' (it is Curley with an 'e' and he is the boss's son) or 'It is Slim's job to skin the mules' (a mule skinner's job is to drive the mules, not skin them).

Higher and foundation tier

You will be entered for the examination at either the foundation or the higher tier.

Foundation tier

The foundation-tier questions are similar to those for the higher tier, but are usually more simply worded, and include some bullet-point guidance. However, the highest grade you can get is a C. The skills you need for either tier are the same, but if you know you are being entered for the foundation tier, be especially careful not to do any of the things listed on p. 71 under the heading 'What you will not get marks for'.

If you are given bullet-point hints, make sure you make use of them. You will probably find it helpful to use them as the basis of your essay plan, although you may need to break them down into further points.

Higher tier

At higher tier you will probably not be given bullet-point hints to help you. If you are not, write some yourself for your essay plan — you need to think carefully about what the question is really asking you to do. It may contain several elements, as explained below.

You may also find that your question is more sophisticated than those on the foundation-tier paper. For example, you may be asked to write about how Steinbeck shows the position of women in American society of the 1930s, rather than being given a question about the character of Curley's wife.

The question

Breaking down the question

If you feel under pressure in the exam, it is tempting to read the question quickly and start writing a response immediately. Stop! First read the passage carefully, noting where it comes in the novel. Then read the question carefully, at least twice, and attempt to break it down into parts to work out exactly what you are being asked to do. This will help to ensure that you really answer the question that is being asked and not the one that you think is being asked or for which you have prepared. You should then reread the passage, underlining or noting lines or phrases that you could use in your answer.

Here is a possible breakdown for the following question, aimed at higher tier. It could well appear in the AQA or WJEC exam. The Edexcel exam essay question is more likely to relate to a theme.

> Consider Slim's role in the novel as a whole and how effectively Steinbeck portrays him.

You could break this down as follows:

- Slim's role on the ranch. He is a highly skilled permanent worker, with some authority.
- How does Slim's role on the ranch reflect his role in the novel? He is presented as an example of the noble working man. The respect he commands for his skills is matched by his personal qualities. Steinbeck uses him as a measure of what is morally right.
- The part Slim plays in the story. He encourages George to talk about himself and Lennie. Curley's suspicion that Slim may be intimate with Curley's wife makes Slim respond angrily to Curley. Curley is cowed by this and takes it out on Lennie. It is then Slim who prevents Curley from getting Lennie fired. Slim also gives Lennie his puppy.
- How effectively does Steinbeck portray him? Steinbeck shows Slim's sympathy towards George and Lennie well, and makes him an effective contrast with Curley. However, he is idealised, and perhaps therefore a little unrealistic as a character. Steinbeck seems to want us to admire him — for example comparing him with a temple dancer. Is this to make a deliberate contrast with the failings and insecurities of the other characters? Does his name imply that there is only a 'slim' chance of finding a man like him?

Interpreting the question

Sometimes the question is open to interpretation. In the example above, the first part could mean more than one thing: it could refer to either Slim's role on the ranch or his role as a character in the novel. If the question were intended to refer only to Slim's role on the ranch, it would probably not say 'his role in the novel as a whole', but we cannot be certain of this. The suggested breakdown of the question given above covers both possibilities and links the two things.

Here is another example question, with several possible interpretations. Here, social context is especially important:

> Discuss the view that the dreams of stardom entertained by Curley's wife are futile.

You could take this to mean that her dreams are futile (pointless) because:

- she has no talent
- she is trapped in her marriage
- a woman in her situation (working-class, uneducated) had little hope of achieving independence in 1930s California
- hardly anyone becomes a Hollywood star
- her dreams seem to make her miserable rather than happy
- she is doomed to die young anyway
- the novel is about disappointment, so no one's dreams come true
- Hollywood stardom is itself empty and pointless

You would be unwise to try to consider all of these options in your essay, so you would need to identify three or four main points you think you can write about well and make it clear in your opening paragraph what these are.

Planning your answers

The section above on breaking down and interpreting the question already goes some way towards explaining how to plan your essay. If you are given bullet-point hints, it will probably be helpful for you to use them as the basis of your plan. If you are given no hints, you need to break down the question as shown above, and use your own breakdown as the basis of your essay plan. If your board is Edexcel and you choose the four-part question, you will probably not need to break each one down.

The form of your plan

You may find it helpful to use a diagram of some sort, perhaps a spider diagram or flow chart. This may help you to keep your mind open to new ideas as you plan, so that you can simply slot them in. You could make a list instead but this is slightly more difficult to add to.

You will probably need to get the important points down on paper in some form before you arrange them. If you have made a spider diagram, arranging them is a simple matter of numbering the branches in the best possible order.

Using an extract

For the first question you will be given an extract to start you off, so make good use of it. Focus on the extract but not to the exclusion of all else. Remember that you can underline and make notes on the extract. Suppose you are again answering the following question:

Discuss the view that the dreams of stardom entertained by Curley's wife are futile.

This time, however, you are also given an extract to start you off, from "'I coulda made somethin' of myself." She said darkly, "Maybe I will yet'" to 'The fingers trailed after her leading wrist, and her little finger stuck out grandly from the rest' (A124–25, P96–97). You could underline phrases in the passage and make notes in the margin to follow up in your essay, as shown in Table 3.

Table 3

Line from text	Comment
'He says he was gonna put me in the movies. Says I was a natural.'	Shows she is gullible and deluded about her talent.
'I never got that letter', she said. 'I always thought my ol' lady stole it.'	Again, gullible, and desperate to believe in her dream.
'Coulda been in the movies, an' had nice clothes — all them nice clothes like they wear.'	More concerned with clothes than acting well.
'An' all them nice clothes like they wear. Because this guy says I was a natural.'	Repetition emphasises her childishness and need to look good and be appreciated.
She made a small grand gesture with her arm and hand to show that she could act. The fingers trailed after her leading wrist, and her little finger stuck out grandly from the rest.	Shows she has no idea what acting involves. Steinbeck uses 'grand' and 'grandly' ironically. He really thinks she is pathetic, not grand.

Structuring your essay

Think in terms of your essay having three sections:

1 beginning (introduction)
2 middle (development)
3 end (conclusion)

You need good ideas to write a good essay, but you also need to demonstrate that you can put them together in a logical order, developing them to reach your conclusion. Here are some hints for each section of the essay.

Beginning (introduction)

Do not spend half your essay time on an introduction and then find you have no time to develop and conclude your essay. This is a common mistake. Instead, limit yourself to an opening paragraph of no more than about 100 words. This should:

- refer to the question and give an initial response to it
- show you have understood it
- show how you intend to answer it, hinting at the views you will put forward
- explain your interpretation, if there is more than one possible interpretation

You may need to give some background here. Do so by all means, but briefly. Do not write 300 words on the position of women in 1930s America.

Middle (development)

This part of the essay is in some ways easier than the other two. If you have made a good plan, you know what you are doing by now and can follow your plan, point by point, presenting your argument with appropriate evidence to back it up.

Your biggest challenge in this part of the essay will probably be to make it flow smoothly from point to point, showing how the points connect. The examiner should never find himself or herself starting to read a paragraph and thinking 'Hang on — how did we get here?'

Part of the secret is to plan properly in the first place, arranging your points in a logical way so that one leads on from the next. However, it is also important to use appropriate link words and phrases. These signpost your ideas, giving the reader an idea of what sort of thing is coming next and how it relates to the previous idea. Look at the words and phrases in Table 4 below, and the ideas they contain. It is important not to overuse any of these words or phrases. Try not to begin any two paragraphs in a row with the same one.

Table 4

Word/phrase	Idea it contains
However Yet	An exception is coming: 'However, Crooks can humble himself if necessary.' 'Yet' can also be used without the comma.
Despite this Nevertheless Nonetheless	Signals an apparent contradiction: 'Despite this, Slim admires George's loyalty.'
On the other hand	Signals a balanced alternative: 'On the other hand, it could be argued that...' Useful for showing you realise that different interpretations of the text are valid.
By contrast	Compares two features. A paragraph on the boss being hard but fair could be followed by: 'By contrast, Curley is anything but fair.'

Word/phrase	Idea it contains
Similarly	Gives a similar example: 'Similarly, Candy speaks well of Crooks.'
Another example	'Another example of Steinbeck slowing down the narrative pace is when the men are waiting for Carlson to shoot Candy's dog.'
In addition	Introduces a point making the previous one even stronger. After a paragraph on how hard life is for the ranch men: 'In addition, the men have little to look forward to.'
Above all	Introduces the most important of several points: 'Above all, George and Lennie look after each other.'

End (conclusion)

The conclusion should draw your arguments to a logical close, but it should not simply repeat them in a different form.

If you have explored two or more sides of an argument, use the conclusion to state which side you personally take. For example 'Having looked at both sides of this question, I feel that…'

Your conclusion should, above all, refer back to the question, showing you have not lost sight of it. In referring back, try to give an overview of your essay. This will help the examiner to see your essay as a whole. Another possible technique is to include a quotation from the text in the last line or couple of lines, especially one that refers to the essay question. For example 'Having considered these possibilities, I believe that Crooks sums up Steinbeck's own views when he says 'Nobody never gets to heaven, and nobody gets no land. It's just in their head.'

Using quotations and referring to the text

It is essential to use quotations and references to the text in your exam essay. This is to provide evidence for your argument. You can express your personal views on the text — in fact, the examiner will be delighted to read something original. However, you must always back them up with evidence.

Separate quotations

The first kind of quotation you can use is the separate quotation. This means making your point, then giving the quotation on a separate line:

Being lonely and a victim of prejudice does not make Curley's wife sympathetic towards Crooks. Rather, she takes the opportunity to exercise power over someone with fewer rights than her:

'I could get you strung up on a tree so easy it ain't even funny.'

Embedded quotations

An embedded quotation is one that runs on from your own words on the same line:

> Curley's helplessness is conveyed by Steinbeck's image of him 'flopping like a fish on a line'.

This kind of quotation works best if the sentence as a whole, with the quotation, is grammatically correct.

Referring to the text

It is not always necessary to use a quotation. If you cannot accurately recall or find the quotation you want, it is often just as good to refer to it:

> When Carlson calls Curley a coward, this is the last straw for Curley. He looks for someone he can attack easily.

This technique is also useful if you need to sum up a lengthy passage:

> George reveals his capacity for moral growth when he tells Slim how he stopped teasing Lennie after he told Lennie to jump into a river and he nearly drowned.

Referring to the author and title

You can refer to Steinbeck either by name (spell it correctly) or as 'the author'. You do not need to give his first name (John). You can also save time by using a simplification of the title. Give the title in full, plus the abbreviation, the first time you use it, for example '*Of Mice and Men* (*Mice*)'. You can then use the one-word version in the rest of your essay.

Writing in an appropriate style

Remember that you are expected to write in an appropriate style for a formal examination essay. Each year, examiners' reports list a range of inappropriate language used by candidates. These examples can make amusing reading, but they have lost the candidates marks. You must write in a suitable **register**. This means:

- *not* using colloquial language or slang (except when quoting dialogue): 'Curley thinks he's well hard, but really he's chicken and his attack on Lennie is out of order.'
- *not* becoming too personal: 'Lennie is like my cousin Wayne, right, who really annoys me because…'
- using suitable phrases for an academic essay. For example, it is better to say 'It could be argued that…', not 'I reckon that…'

Grade ***booster***

To check on how good you are at embedding quotations, read your whole sentence (containing the quotation) out to someone who has not read the novel. See if they can tell where Steinbeck's words begin and end. If not, you've integrated his words smoothly.

The first person ('I')

Grade *booster*

Avoid beginning your essay by spelling out exactly what you intend to do ('In this essay I will show that…'): just get on with it!

At one time it was thought to be a bad thing to write essays in the first person (using 'I'). Now this is acceptable, although you should not do it all the way through the essay. You could use it to your advantage, especially in the opening and closing paragraphs, where you preview your argument and then give your considered opinion.

Some use of the first person can help to show the examiner that you have really engaged with the text and are giving a personal response rather than just repackaging what your teacher has told you, or what you have read.

Responding to an extract

Questions based on an extract invite you to make a close study of it. At higher-tier level, you are especially likely to be asked to discuss 'how Steinbeck presents' a character. This refers to Steinbeck's style, so you should not just write about the character in a general way. Instead, you should discuss such features as:

- the dialogue Steinbeck gives the character — for example, Curley's wife's childish repetition of 'nice clothes' when she speaks to Lennie
- any adverbs Steinbeck uses to qualify the way the character speaks
- any actions, however small — for example, Candy nervously scratching his cheek, indicating his uneasiness
- any direct description of the character — for example, Slim's hands being compared with those of a 'temple dancer' or Crooks being 'a proud, aloof man'

Review your learning

(Answers are given on p. 86.)

1. What are the two ways to use quotations?
2. What other kind of textual evidence can you provide?
3. What should you do to the question before attempting to answer it?
4. What should your introduction and conclusion ideally mention?

More interactive questions and answers online.

Assessment Objectives and skills

Assessment Objectives

The examiner marking your exam essay will be trying to give you marks, but will only be able to do so if you fulfil the key Assessment Objectives for English literature:

- AO1: respond to texts critically and imaginatively; select and evaluate relevant textual detail to illustrate and support interpretations.
- AO2: explain how language, structure and form contribute to writers' presentation of ideas, themes and settings.
- AO4: relate texts to their social, cultural and historical contexts; explain how texts have been influential and significant to self and other readers in different contexts and at different times.

How these apply to different exam boards

Find out from your teacher which exam board your school or college is using. Then you can check below to see which AOs need your special attention.

- AO1 is important for all exam boards.
- AO2 is important for AQA, WJEC and CCEA, but is not tested for Edexcel.
- AO3 is not listed here as it relates to comparing texts, and you will not have to do this for *Of Mice and Men*.
- AO4 is relevant to all boards (except CCEA), as they regard *Of Mice and Men* as an 'other cultures' text. It is especially important for Edexcel.

Breaking down the Assessment Objectives

AO1: respond to texts critically and imaginatively; select a nd evaluate relevant textual detail to illustrate and support interpretations

- **respond to texts critically:** you must say what you think of the novel and why. You are being asked to **evaluate** it. Of course, this involves realising that the author has made choices and giving your

views on how effective they are. For example, you might write, 'Some critics think that Steinbeck drops too many hints about the tragedy that is to come — for example, in the shooting of Candy's old dog. Personally, I feel these hints add to a sense of fate being at work, as if the tragedy cannot be avoided.'

- **...and imaginatively:** you have to use your imagination to consider possible reasons for Steinbeck's choice of details and phrasing, and for what the characters say and do. This involves 'reading between the lines'. For example, Crooks says to Lennie, 'You got no right to come in my room.' If you take this at face value, you might just think that Crooks is unfriendly. However, if you use your imagination you can begin to understand his mixed feelings about accepting a white man's company. This AO also requires an awareness that there is no single correct way to interpret the novel. For example, readers differ in the degree of sympathy they think Curley's wife deserves.

- **select and evaluate relevant textual detail:** this means providing short quotations from the text, or referring to details in the text, to support your views. Evaluating them means analysing their meaning and effectiveness. To support your assessment of Curley's wife, you might write:

It could be argued that Curley's wife deserves to die. She is cruel to Crooks, threatening him with lynching. However, I see her as a victim herself. Her desperate insistence 'I coulda made somethin' of myself...Maybe I will yet' is pathetic and demands our sympathy.

This uses details and a quotation as evidence.

AO2: explain how language, structure and form contribute to writers' presentation of ideas, themes and settings

- **...language, structure and form:** the word 'language' refers to Steinbeck's use of words. For example, describing Slim, he says 'His hands, large and lean, were as delicate in their action as those of a temple dancer' (A56, P37). There are many other ways in which Steinbeck could have made the point that Slim's sensitivity and grace show in his hands. Using this simile of a temple dancer contributes to this **idea** by hinting at something holy and at the respect that others show Slim. 'Structure' refers to the overall shape of the novel, as discussed in the *Plot and structure* section. Remember that the novel begins and ends in the same place. The word 'form' is more vague. For example, in *Of Mice and Men* it could be taken to refer to Steinbeck's attempt to write 'a playable novel. Written in novel form but so scened and set that it can be played as it stands.'

- **ideas, themes and settings:** we have looked at the 'idea' of Slim's grace and sensitivity; 'themes' have their own section in this guide; 'settings' refers to the places in which events take place, such as the pool by the river, the bunk house, and the barn.

AO4: relate texts to their social, cultural and historical contexts; explain how texts have been influential and significant to self and other readers in different contexts and at different times

- **relate texts to their social, cultural and historical contexts:** this means showing understanding of the influences on Steinbeck when he wrote the novel. George and Lennie are in many ways typical of the poor, underprivileged, travelling farm workers of the Depression (see *Context* section). This is part of the social and historical context. The fact that Curley's wife — like most uneducated American women of the time — has little hope of fulfilling any personal ambitions is part of the cultural context. The prejudice against Crooks could be seen as cultural and historical. The literary tradition is less important. At GCSE you will not be expected to compare Steinbeck's novel with others or to suggest which earlier novelists influenced him. However, the fact that it is a fairly realistic novel is significant. Many earlier novels were less realistic and few authors considered the poor worth writing about.
- **…how texts have been influential and significant to self and other readers in different contexts and at different times:** this means showing your awareness of why a text has lasting appeal and how it can be interpreted in different ways at different times or in different places.

What you will not get marks for

The Assessment Objectives tell you what you *will* get marks for. It is also important to know what you *will not* get marks for:

- **Retelling the story.** You can be certain that the examiner marking your essay already knows the plot of *Of Mice and Men*. He or she may have taught the novel, perhaps for several years, and will not want to be told the story again. The examiner follows a mark scheme and will probably be referring to 'grade descriptors' — these outline the features to be expected from essays at each of the grades. A key feature of the lowest grades, as identified by the grade descriptors, is 'retelling the story' — so do not do it!
- **Quoting long passages.** You will waste time and gain no marks by quoting long passages from the novel. Use your judgement, but it will probably never be necessary for you to quote more than two sentences at a time.

- **Identifying figures of speech or other features.** You will never gain marks simply by identifying images such as similes or metaphors. Similarly, you will gain no marks for pointing out that 'Steinbeck uses a lot of adverbs in this passage.' You will only gain marks by identifying these features and then saying why the author has used them and how effective you think they are. See, for example, the comments on Steinbeck's description of Slim under AO2 above.
- **Giving unsubstantiated opinions.** The examiner will be keen to give you marks for your opinions but only if they are supported by reasoned argument and references to the text. Therefore, you will get no marks for writing 'Everyone thinks that Lennie is completely stupid but I don't. George, on the other hand…' You will get marks for:

> It is easy to dismiss Lennie as lacking any intelligence. However, he does show a kind of intelligence in his understanding of people. For example, he senses when George is feeling guilty about being 'mean' to him and uses this to manipulate George. Steinbeck writes: 'Lennie avoided the bait. He had sensed his advantage.' A little later, Lennie is said to speak 'craftily'.

This gives a reasoned and insightful view, backed up by evidence from the text. It also shows an awareness of other possible viewpoints.

Exam board summary

Importance of Assessment Objectives for each board

Table 5 summarises the percentage weighting for each Assessment Objective for the 'other cultures' novel question (including *Of Mice and Men*) in each of the exam boards. They add up to different amounts because the 'other cultures' novel section of the exam is only one part of the exam.

Table 5

	AO1	AO2	AO4
AQA	15.0	15.0	10.0
WJEC	8.16	3.5	9.33
Edexcel	25.0	—	25.0
CCEA	12.5	12.5	—

Notes on individual boards

AQA

You have 45 minutes for the 'Exploring cultures' section. There is one two-part question. Part (a) is on a quoted passage; part (b) develops the ideas in (a), asking you to comment on the novel as a whole. For example, part (a) might ask you to focus on how a particular character is portrayed in the passage, with part (b) asking you to write about how that character is used to develop a particular theme. There is no choice of question. You can take your text into the exam.

WJEC

Question (a) asks you to comment on a given passage. You then have a choice of questions, (b) or (c), which are on the novel as a whole and do not necessarily relate closely to the quoted passage. You are recommended to take 20 minutes on (a) and 40 minutes on (b) or (c). The exam is 'closed text': you cannot take your text into the exam.

Edexcel

The exam lasts 1 hour 45 minutes. You should spend half of this on the 'other cultures' section. You can choose between two questions. The first has four parts. The first two parts are based on characters and themes in a given passage, and the other two parts ask you to look at the same characters and themes elsewhere in the novel. The second question is a theme-based or character-based question with bullet-point hints for *both* tiers. For foundation tier the tasks are simpler. You can take your text into the exam.

CCEA

The exam lasts 1 hour. There is a choice of two questions on each text. The exam is closed-text: you cannot take your text into the exam.

Review your learning

(Answers are given on p. 86.)

1. What four things should you avoid because they waste time and earn no marks?
2. What does 'respond to texts critically' mean?
3. What does 'evaluate relevant textual detail' mean?
4. *Of Mice and Men* begins and ends with the setting of the pool by the river. What aspect of the novel does this relate to?
5. *Of Mice and Men* is regarded as an 'other cultures' novel by all exam boards. Which Assessment Objective does this relate to?

More interactive questions and answers online.

Four sample essays are provided below — grade C and grade A* answers to two different types of questions: a character-based question and a theme-based question. It is suggested that you read the grade C essays first and see how you could improve on them. Then read the A* essays. However, remember that there could be many different good approaches to the same essay. These sample essays are not meant to be learned by heart and reproduced in the exam.

Question 1

This question is in the style of the AQA higher tier, but it is similar to a WJEC-style question.

> Read the passage in Section 2 which introduces Curley's wife, from 'Both men glanced up' to 'and she hurried away'. Then answer the questions which follow.
> (a) How does Steinbeck use details in this passage to show what Curley's wife is like?
> (b) Discuss the way in which Steinbeck presents women in the novel as a whole.

Grade C response

(a) Curley's wife is described as having 'full, rouged lips' and her eyes are 'heavily made up'. These details suggest that she wants to appear sexy. Her red fingernails especially show that she has made an effort with her appearance.**1** Her shoes (mules) seem more suitable for going to a party than walking around a ranch. The fact that her voice has 'a nasal, brittle quality' does not in itself mean that she is a bad person, but this description is unattractive, as if she is common, not elegant like she would like to be.**2**

George looks away from her at first because he feels awkward about looking at her because she is the boss's wife.**3** The fact that she leans against the door frame shows that she isn't looking very hard for Curley.**4** Maybe she just wants something to do, or an excuse to go in the bunk house. Also, leaning like this pushes her forward which shows off her bust.**5**

When she 'bridles' because Lennie is looking at her this suggests that she is angry

---

1 Good point, but her nails also suggest danger, and that she has time on her hands (almost literally!).

2 Slightly clumsy expression, and not enough analysis of the words used. 'Brittle' could suggest fragility as well.

3 She's the boss's *son's* wife, and perhaps he also disapproves of her.

4 Good interpretation, but this is an opportunity to mention that she may be bored. This could link to the time she spends on her appearance.

5 True, but further comment is needed on why she might want to do this.

or embarrassed, so perhaps she doesn't want to be looked at after all. However, this doesn't stop her being playful in a flirty kind of way.**6** This changes when Slim tells her that he saw Curley going into their house.**7**

(b) The only female character in the novel is Curley's wife, so we have to accept the way Steinbeck shows her as being what he thinks of women.[1] Other women are mentioned, but only prostitutes and George's aunt. The men on the ranch all fancy[2] Curley's wife, which is a big problem for Curley. He's really jealous. Steinbeck shows her to be a 'tart'[3] pointing out that she wears a lot of make-up and has sausage hair.[4] Candy says that she's pretty but that 'she got the eye'. He adds that she is 'a tart'. Steinbeck also describes her speaking 'playfully' and writes 'She smiled archly and twitched her body'.[5]

Steinbeck has already shown how women cause trouble. In Weed, which is where George and Lennie used to work before they came to Salinas, Lennie touched a girl's dress and she screamed and tried to make out that he had tried to rape her. So they had to hide in a ditch all day to escape. George doesn't want this to happen again, because he thinks a lot of Lennie even though he is not very bright and does 'bad things', and he wants to protect him. George also warns us that Curley's wife is going to cause trouble.**6**

These hints are developed when violence breaks out because of Curley's jealous suspicions of his wife. Curley thinks that Slim has been with his wife, which he hasn't, and this makes Slim angry, which makes Curley want to pick on someone. He tries to have a go**7** at Carlson, who threatens to kick his head in, so Curley takes it out on Lennie. Curley's wife is the cause of all this so the message is again that she is 'trouble'.**8**

Slim is nice to her, although even he only refers to her looks: 'Hi, Good-lookin'.' George is a good man but still calls her a 'tramp' and comments 'So that's what Curley picks for a wife.' This shows his disapproval.**9**

We meet Curley's wife again in person when she invites herself into the bunk house. The image of her built up so far now becomes even more negative. However, we do see something more of her. First, she has the intelligence to guess why the men avoid her. We see how limited her life is, which may make us sympathise with her. She is apparently not happy with Curley:**10**

'Sure I gotta husban'. You all seen him. Swell guy, ain't he? Spends all his time sayin' what he's gonna do to guys he don't like, and he don't like nobody. Think I'm gonna stay in that two-by-four house and listen how Curley's gonna lead with his left twice, and then bring in the ol' right cross? "One-two," he says. "Jus' the ol' one-two an' he'll go down."'

---

6 Better to say 'playfully flirtatious'.
7 Valid observation, but some analysis is needed. Overall comment: some good observation but not enough attention given to possible interpretations, context and actual words used.

1 Not necessarily true.
2 Inappropriate language.
3 He does not show that she *is* 'a tart' — more that the men think she is.
4 Poorly worded.
5 Good details, but no explanation of their relevance.

6 This paragraph is badly placed structurally. It also slips into retelling the story, then into irrelevance (George and Lennie).

7 Inappropriate language.
8 More retelling and irrelevance in this paragraph.

9 Good points but insufficiently developed.

10 Good points but the quotation used is too long.

11 Some good points but not focused on Steinbeck's presentation. Also, some poor expression: 'greatly lessened', 'strung up'. A short quotation would help.

12 Inappropriate language and poor expression.
13 A good point but needs development and a short quotation.
14 Not necessarily true.

15 Weak conclusion. It starts with an unsubstantiated claim about Steinbeck. There is clumsy expression (repetition of 'shows') and it is inaccurate to call Curley's wife 'empty-headed' (the candidate has already credited her with some intelligence, and she does have ambitions). The last sentence is idle speculation: the characters do not exist outside the novel.

1 Awareness of literary context.
2 Awareness of symbolism, with personal interpretation.
3 Suggests alternative interpretations, one based on context.

4 Interpretation of physical details.

She is bored by Curley's conversation. She admits that she's come to talk to Candy, Crooks and Lennie because she is lonely, but her dislike of their unfriendliness makes her insult them by calling them 'a bunch of bindle stiffs'. If we feel sympathy towards her, it is greatly lessened by the way she threatens to get Crooks strung up.**11**

Steinbeck tells us more about Curley's wife in her final scene, when she confides in Lennie. She insists: 'I coulda made somethin' of myself.' She spills out her dreams of stardom, telling Lennie how one man wanted her to join a travelling show but she was too young, and then how another promised to get her into the movies in Hollywood. But her ambitions are pathetic. She thinks that her mum stole her letter from the Hollywood man, which shows she'll believe anything.**12** And she seems just into the 'nice clothes' that she could wear. The gesture she makes to display her acting talents shows that she thinks she could be a great actress.**13** When she dies, she is just pathetic. Steinbeck has made no effort whatsoever to make us like her. In fact, the final comment on her comes from Candy, who dismisses her as a 'lousy tart'. This would seem to be Steinbeck's own view.**14**

I think that Steinbeck probably didn't like women very much and thought they were shallow and just more trouble than they were worth. This shows in the way he shows Curley's wife as being empty-headed and vain about her ambitions. It also shows in the way he doesn't even bother giving her a name. I also think that if she had been given a chance she could have got a better husband and perhaps even got to Hollywood in the way she wanted.**15**

Grade A* response

(a) Steinbeck introduces Curley's wife in a way which reflects the fact that he originally conceived of this novel being written for the stage.**1** He describes how she cuts off the light by standing in the doorway, casting a shadow literally and metaphorically, as if she is denying George and Lennie life and escape from their situation.**2** He presents her in quite a complex way. She is 'a girl' rather than a woman, which could suggest that she is young, or merely that Steinbeck, like many men of the time, sees women in this way.**3**

Steinbeck spends some time simply describing Curley's wife's physical appearance, as if in a stage direction. He portrays a young woman who cares a great deal about her appearance and must spend a lot of time on it. Her lips are 'full', suggesting sensuality, while her rouge and heavy make-up suggest that she wants to make an impression on the men on the ranch.**4** On the other hand, this in itself could suggest her insecurity, as could the 'brittle' quality of her voice, which suggests that she is fragile rather than merely lacking in grace. Her red nails suggest danger, and this colour is echoed in her footwear, which is completely inappropriate for the ranch and suggests the dreams of film stardom that she eventually confides in Lennie later in the book.**5**

She seems to be ambivalent in her attitude towards the men. On the one hand she stays longer than she needs to if she is really looking for Curley; on the other, she is slightly uncomfortable about Lennie staring at her in a way that suggests his attraction to her ('she bridled a little'). The fact that she notices at all suggests that she is attuned to the effect she has on men.**6**

6 Good analysis of character.

Steinbeck makes it clear that there is something playful and therefore potentially dangerous about Curley's wife. She says 'playfully' that she will look somewhere else for her husband. Her 'arch' smile suggests something mischievous and slightly superior in her attitude, and the 'twitching' of her body appears to be flirtatious.**7**

7 Sensitive analysis of Steinbeck's words.

Her attitude when she hears that Curley has gone into the house is in contrast. We are not told why she is 'apprehensive' and why she 'hurries' away, but these words reveal tensions in the marriage, suggesting that Steinbeck wants us to have some sympathy with her plight.**8**

8 Awareness of author's possible purpose.

(b) *Of Mice and Men* is set almost entirely on the ranch, and this is a man's world. It follows that Steinbeck's presentation of women is not wide-ranging. However, even given these limitations, his presentation of women seems unnecessarily negative.**1**

1 Strong introduction — refers to the question, making an important observation on the setting and giving an initial opinion which is developed in the essay.

The only female character in the novel is Curley's wife. Other women are mentioned, but she is the only one to appear in person. As the only female character, and as one who plays such a major role in the plot, the way in which Steinbeck presents her is crucial.**2** Yet she is portrayed in a rather two-dimensional way.**3** It is perhaps not surprising that the ranch men have a stereotypical view of her. When Candy describes her to George, he says that she's pretty, but that 'she got the eye' — meaning that she takes a sexual interest in men other than Curley. He adds disapprovingly that she is 'a tart'. When she appears soon after this, Steinbeck's presentation of her reinforces Candy's view. She blocks out the light as she looks into the bunk house. As Steinbeck uses light to symbolise goodness, her blocking it out warns us that she is bad — or at least that she will lead to bad things happening.**4** Moreover, she is heavily made up and her hair hangs 'in little rolled clusters, like sausages'. This is an unflattering description. Steinbeck also describes her speaking 'playfully' and writes 'She smiled archly and twitched her body.' These details suggest that she is flirtatious.**5**

2 Shows awareness of the role of Curley's wife.

3 Makes a critical judgement, backed up by the rest of the paragraph.

4 Sensitive appraisal of Steinbeck's technique, focused on the question.

5 Good use of short quotations with an explanation of their significance.

Slim is pleasant to her, although even he only refers to her looks: 'Hi, Good-lookin'.' George, whose opinion we are generally supposed to respect, calls her a 'tramp' (almost a prostitute) and comments 'So that's what Curley picks for a wife.' The word 'that's' suggests that she is treated as a thing, not a person. This is emphasised

6 Relevant focus on detail. Good point about her being unnamed, which is well explained.

by the fact that Steinbeck never gives her a name. He wants us to see that on the ranch she is not treated as an individual in her own right.**6**

By describing the incident in Weed, Steinbeck warns us that women cause trouble. Through George, he further warns us that Curley's wife is going to cause trouble:

'She's gonna make a mess. They's gonna be a bad mess about her. She's a jail bait all set on the trigger.'

7 Relevant reference to Steinbeck's technique, with good use of a short quotation and a critical comment ('heavy hints').

These rather heavy hints are developed when violence breaks out in the third section because of Curley's jealous suspicions of her. His wife is not present, but the message again is that she is 'trouble'.**7**

8 Close observation of text and perceptive comment.

We meet Curley's wife again in person when she invites herself into Crooks's room (Section 4). There is little here to dispel the negative image of her built up so far. Again, she is heavily made up and her slightly parted lips suggest sexuality.**8**

However, we do see something more of her. First, she has the intelligence to guess why the men avoid her:

9 Good use of short quotations, here and below.

'Ever' one of you's scared the rest is goin' to get something on you.'**9**

We also get a glimpse of how limited her life is, which may make us sympathise with her. She is apparently not happy with Curley:

'Sure I gotta husban'. You all seen him. Swell guy, ain't he?'

She is bored by his talk of what he's going to do to men he doesn't like. She admits that she's come to talk to Candy, Crooks and Lennie because she is lonely, but her resentment at their unfriendliness makes her insult them, calling them 'a bunch of bindle stiffs'. If we feel sympathy towards her, it is likely to be wiped out by her treatment of Crooks. When he tries to make her leave his room, she threatens to get him lynched:

'I could get you strung up on a tree so easy it ain't even funny.'

Steinbeck gives us further insight into Curley's wife in her final scene, when she confides in Lennie. She insists 'I coulda made somethin' of myself.' She spills out her dreams of stardom, telling Lennie how one man wanted her to join a travelling show, and then how another promised to get her 'in pitchers' in Hollywood. But her ambitions come across as pathetic. Her conviction that the man's letter must have been stolen shows her gullibility. Her repeated mention of the 'nice clothes' she could have worn makes her sound like a child. The 'small grand gesture' she makes to display her acting ability shows that she is deluded about her talents, and that Steinbeck wants us to see this: his use of the word 'grand' is ironic. When she dies, we may feel a little sympathy, but she is at best a pathetic figure, not a tragic one. Steinbeck has made no effort to make us more sympathetic towards her. In fact, the final comment on her comes from Candy, who dismisses her as a 'lousy tart'. Steinbeck offers no other view to balance this.**10**

The other women in the novel appear only in being mentioned by the men. Lennie's Aunt Clara apparently cared about him, but appears in his hallucinations at the end to tell him off. Susy, the woman who runs a local brothel and is described by Whit, apparently has a sense of humour. Whit describes the brothel appreciatively. It seems as if the prostitutes are given more respect than Curley's wife, whom Curley abandons for them on a Saturday night.**11**

I feel, therefore, that Steinbeck's presentation of women shows in a very poor light in *Of Mice and Men*. The only woman we meet in person is presented as shallow, deluded and pathetic, even in death lacking the nobility to be tragic. We hardly see her as a real person, and certainly not as one to respect, however much we may sympathise with her plight. It seems that in this novel, women are mostly a source of trouble — from the girl in Weed to Curley's wife. The only acceptable role is either as the motherly old aunt or as the prostitute.**12**

10 This paragraph analyses Curley's wife's scene with Lennie, observing and interpreting details in the text. It also shows awareness of the author's intentions and technique (irony).

11 Useful comparison between the presentation of Curley's wife and the prostitutes.

12 Refers to the question and gives a personal opinion, backed up by a summary that avoids simple repetition. The last sentence neatly spells out the key idea developed in the essay.

Question 2

This could be an Edexcel question (foundation or higher) or, without the bullet-points hints, an AQA (b) or WJEC (b or c) question. AQA would normally give two bullet hints for foundation tier. For AQA or WJEC the foundation version might be worded more simply.

> How does Steinbeck present the theme of loneliness in *Of Mice and Men*?
>
> Write about:
> - which characters are lonely and why
> - how Steinbeck shows their loneliness
> - what conclusions Steinbeck seems to reach about loneliness.

Grade C response

Steinbeck writes about three lonely characters: Candy, Crooks and Curley's wife. We find out early in the novel that loneliness is important when Lennie persuades George to tell him again about their 'dream farm':

'Guys like us, that work on ranches, are the loneliest guys in the world. They got no family. They don't belong no place.'**1**

George then says he and Lennie have escaped this fate. They have each other:

'We got somebody to talk to that gives a damn about us.'

1 Good use of a short quotation, but still not a strong introduction. No reference to the question or preview of what is to follow.

2 Inappropriate language.

Candy is the first lonely character. He is a lonely old man. He is old and therefore not valued highly. He also misses out on friendship in work. Having lost a hand on the ranch, he can only work as a swamper, a solitary job. His loneliness is shown by how he is dead keen**2** to talk to George. As soon as he hears about the 'dream farm' planned by George and Lennie, he gets excited and offers to help buy the farm. He says:

3 Potentially useful quotation but without any explanation of its relevance.

'I ain't got no relatives nor nothing.'[3]

Steinbeck also underlines Candy's loneliness with his old sheepdog. Candy is reluctant to let Carlson shoot the dog, despite its age, because the dog is his best mate. Candy says 'I had him so long'. When Carlson continues to talk of shooting the dog, Candy looks around 'helplessly' and speaks 'hopelessly'.**4** Later, Candy tells Curley's wife that he is no longer alone:

4 Poor expression (first sentence), inappropriate language (second sentence) and the point of the quotations is not explained.

'An' we got fren's, that's what we got.'

But he is condemned to loneliness again when Curley's wife dies. He bitterly addresses her dead body, blaming her for ruining their dream. It's all a bit ironic because Lennie was only in the barn because of his puppy, which he got from Slim, and now it's dead, so Curley's wife (who is also lonely) got chatting to him.**5**

5 Irrelevance and inappropriate language.

Crooks is another lonely man. He is the only black man in the area. We learn early on that the boss takes his anger out on Crooks, but we only really see how lonely he is in Section 4, which focuses closely on him.

Steinbeck rarely comments directly on characters, but he does on Crooks:

'This room was swept and fairly neat, for Crooks was a proud, aloof man.'

It is this pride that makes him more lonely. Shunned because of his colour, he is determined not to seek white men's company. When Lennie tries to befriend him, he resists at first, saying he wants to be alone:**6**

6 Good point about Crooks.

'You got no right to come in my room. This here's my room. Nobody got any right in here but me.'

Nonetheless, he is eventually grateful for someone to talk to. He reveals that he takes pride in not being 'a southern negro', meaning that his family has no recent history of slavery. There had been a lot of slavery in America, but not much in California. It was very unjust and they had to work on the cotton fields in bad conditions.**7**

7 True but irrelevant.

Crooks envies Lennie his friendship with George, which is why he tells him George might not come back. But then he shows his own loneliness:

'S'pose you didn't have nobody. S'pose you couldn't go into the bunk house and play rummy 'cause you was black. How'd you like that? S'pose you had to sit out here an' read books. Sure you could play horseshoes till it got dark, but then you got to read books. Books ain't no good. A guy needs somebody — to be near him.' He whined, 'A guy goes nuts if he ain't got nobody. Don't make no difference who the guy is, long's he's with you. I tell ya,' he cried, 'I tell ya a guy gets too lonely an' he gets sick.'**8**

8 Quotation much too long.

Curley's wife is lonely because she is the only woman in a man's world.**9** She has recently married a man who regards her as a trophy rather than a wife. Curley's wife's flirting may be her response to loneliness. Certainly it is loneliness and boredom that make her visit Crooks. She admits that she has nothing better to do and no one better to talk to:

9 Simplistic.

'Standin' here talkin' to a bunch of bindle stiffs…an' likin' it because they ain't nobody else.'

But her loneliness just makes her bitter towards these men, even though she has something in common with them. So she remains locked into it. This is made all the more sure by thinking that she should have been a star.**10**

10 Almost a very good point but lacks proper explanation.

Of Mice and Men is full of lonely no-hopers. No one finds a real friend — George has to kill his only friend, although he can at least make sure that Lennie dies happy. The only sign of hope at the end of the novel is that Slim is sympathetic towards George and may befriend him.**11**

11 Phrase 'no-hopers' inappropriate. This conclusion discusses the plot rather than Steinbeck's *presentation* of the theme.

Grade A* response

Steinbeck presents loneliness as a central theme in *Of Mice and Men,* one which relates closely to both the other major themes of the novel: broken dreams and prejudice. Steinbeck explores the theme of loneliness through three main characters: Candy, Crooks and Curley's wife. However, George and Lennie also play a part in this theme as they demonstrate the alternative to loneliness.**1** The theme is stated early in the novel, when Lennie persuades George to tell him again about their 'dream farm':

1 Refers to the question and shows a subtle grasp of the interconnections between themes. Previews what is to follow.

'Guys like us, that work on ranches, are the loneliest guys in the world. They got no family. They don't belong no place.'

George then recounts how he and Lennie have escaped this fate:

'We got somebody to talk to that gives a damn about us.'**2**

2 Good use of short quotations, identifying how Steinbeck identifies the theme.

George and Lennie have each other. As George later tells Slim, 'We kinda look after each other'. Slim comments that few men travel together. We learn from this that what George has said is true: loneliness is the norm for men like this.**3** Candy is a lonely man. He is old and therefore not valued highly. He also misses out on

3 Evidence followed by what it shows us.

the camaraderie of work. Having lost a hand on the ranch, he can only work as a swamper, a solitary job. His loneliness is shown by his eagerness to talk to George. As soon as he hears about the 'dream farm' planned by George and Lennie, he speaks 'excitedly' and offers his compensation money to help buy the farm. His underlying reason becomes clearer when he offers to leave his share to them in his will:

4 Good use of a quotation, with its significance properly explained.

'I ain't got no relatives nor nothing.'**4**

Steinbeck also underlines Candy's loneliness by showing his attachment to his old sheepdog. Candy is reluctant to let Carlson shoot the dog, despite its age, because in effect the dog is his only friend. As Candy says 'I had him so long.' When Carlson continues to talk of shooting the dog, Candy looks around 'helplessly' and speaks 'hopelessly'. These adverbs convey his sadness at the loss of his old friend.**5** When Candy tells Curley's wife that he is not a 'bindle stiff', an important point he makes is that he is no longer alone:

5 Close analysis of the text, showing how Steinbeck *presents* the theme.

6 Close analysis of the text, showing how Steinbeck *presents* the theme.

'An' we got fren's, that's what we got.'**6**

He is condemned to loneliness once more when Curley's wife dies. He bitterly addresses her dead body, blaming her for ruining their dream. He is 'blinded with tears' when he thinks of how it could have been:

'I could of hoed in the garden and washed dishes for them guys.'

His dream of friendship in old age has been shattered.

Crooks is perhaps even lonelier than Candy. He is a black man living in a period in American history when extreme racial prejudice was widespread and a black man could not expect equality.**7** Moreover, he is almost the only black man in the area. We learn early on that the boss routinely takes his anger out on Crooks, but we only really see the extent of his loneliness in Section 4, which focuses closely on Crooks.

7 Appropriate brief reference to relevant background, addressing Assessment Objective 4.

Steinbeck rarely comments directly on characters, but he comments on Crooks. He presents Crooks's room as a reflection of its owner:**8**

8 Perceptive comment on Steinbeck's writing technique.

'This room was swept and fairly neat, for Crooks was a proud, aloof man.'

It is this pride that intensifies his loneliness. Shunned because of his colour, he is proudly determined not to seek company that is not freely granted. When Lennie tries to befriend him, he resists at first, insisting on his right to be alone:

'You got no right to come in my room. This here's my room. Nobody got any right in here but me.'

Nonetheless, he eventually softens, grateful for someone to talk to. He reveals that he takes pride in not being 'a southern negro', meaning that his family has no recent history of slavery. Ironically, if he had lived in the South, he would have been part of a community.**9**

Crooks envies Lennie his friendship with George, which is why he taunts him with the idea that George might not come back.**10** But then he reveals his own loneliness:

'A guy goes nuts if he ain't got nobody. Don't make no difference who the guy is, long's he's with you. I tell ya…a guy gets too lonely an' he gets sick.'

This seems to be a central message of the novel.**11**

Curley's wife is lonely for other reasons. She is the only woman in a male environment and has recently married a man who regards her as a trophy rather than a human being and partner. Steinbeck emphasises this by never showing them together in the novel. Curley's wife's flirtatiousness may be her response to loneliness. Certainly it is loneliness, together with the boredom that goes with it, that makes her visit Crooks's room. She admits that she has nothing better to do and no one better to talk to:

'Standin' here talkin' to a bunch of bindle stiffs…an' likin' it because they ain't nobody else.'

Sadly, her loneliness makes her bitter rather than compassionate towards these men with whom she has something in common, so she remains locked into it.**12** This is made all the more sure by her deluded belief that she has wasted talent:

'I coulda made somethin' of myself.'

Steinbeck compares the loneliness of Candy, Crooks and Curley's wife with the friendship of George and Lennie. Nonetheless, I feel that the theme of loneliness is presented very pessimistically. Each of the three lonely characters has a brief glimpse of intimacy in the company of Lennie, but is then returned to loneliness. In the case of Curley's wife, the glimpse ends in death. No one in the novel finds a lasting friend, and George is obliged to kill his only friend, although he can at least ensure that Lennie dies happy. The only glimmer of hope at the end of the novel is that Slim is sympathetic towards George and may befriend him.**13**

9 Appropriate brief reference to relevant background, addressing Assessment Objective 4.

10 Sensitive response to the text, reading between the lines.

11 Strong, clear personal statement justifying the quote.

12 Sensitive personal response showing engagement with the text.

13 Strong conclusion summing up the argument and stating a personal judgement.

Answers

Answers to *Review your learning* questions.

Context (p. 13)

1 After the Wall Street Crash, people were wary of investing in business, so few new businesses started and employers tried to cut costs by reducing their workforce.
2 Poor farm workers from Oklahoma, including those who had owned land now worthless, went to California. This flooded the wage market, so bosses could keep wages low.
3 There was no established class system in America and there was land available for people to farm.
4 Curley's wife's wants to be a Hollywood film star.
5 You could consider the position of immigrants in Britain, both legal and illegal. Some people claim that the British economy would collapse without the latter because they will work for so little money.

Plot and structure (p. 25)

1 George is complaining about the bus driver making them walk so far.
2 George warns Lennie to stay away from Curley and his wife.
3 The novel begins on a Thursday evening and ends late on Sunday afternoon.
4 Consider Steinbeck's description of places, such as the pool by the river, and of people — for example of Slim (hands like 'a temple dancer') and Curley's wife (hair 'like sausages').
5 This is up to you, but the novel would not be a tragedy if they escaped.

Characterisation (p. 39)

1 Lennie almost drowned when George told him to jump into a river.
2 a Curley's wife b Candy c Slim
3 a George to Lennie. George sometimes gets frustrated by having to look after Lennie, but he puts up with it because they are friends and he feels a responsibility towards Lennie.
   b Slim to George. This shows that Slim values moral goodness more highly than intellect. As Steinbeck sets Slim up as a role model, this suggests that Steinbeck shares this view.

c Crooks to Lennie. Harsh experience has persuaded Crooks that his own life is hopeless. He feels angry and bitter when he meets someone who believes in something he would like to believe in himself but cannot.

Themes (p. 50)

1 The themes identified are loneliness, friendship, shattered dreams, injustice and the working man.
2 Candy, Crooks and Curley's wife most reflect the theme of loneliness.
3 Crooks is a 'proud, aloof man'.
4 Slim represents 'the noble working man'.
5 You could make a case for any of the themes in this guide. If, for example, you chose friendship, you could argue:
   - the two main characters are friends
   - other people comment on the friendship — Slim in a positive way
   - the 'dream farm' is as much about friendship as independence and rabbits
   - the act towards which the whole novel builds — George's mercy killing of Lennie — is an act of friendship

Style (p. 59)

1 The main setting is the ranch.
2 ● The settings can be shown easily on stage, which is why we never see the men working in the fields with mules and horses.
   - Every section begins with a descriptive passage that could easily be taken as directions to a set designer.
   - Much of the story is told through action and dialogue, as in a play.
   - Steinbeck reveals characters largely through what they say and do, and what others say about them. He hardly ever makes a direct comment on a character. A rare example is when he says 'Crooks was a proud, aloof man.'
3 Steinbeck uses a lot of adverbs. He uses them to describe the way a character speaks or acts. For example, 'Lennie looked timidly', '"Hide in the brush," said Lennie slowly.'
4 Every section begins with a description of a scene.
5 Steinbeck uses colloquial language, including slang, and spells words to reflect the way the characters would actually say them.

Tackling the exam (p. 68)

1 Quotations can be separate or embedded (run on from your own words).
2 References to events or passages that you do not quote directly.
3 Break down the question and consider whether there are different ways to interpret it.
4 The introduction and conclusion should mention the question.

Assessment Objectives and skills (p. 73)

1 Do not:
- retell the story
- quote long passages
- identify figures of speech without discussing their effectiveness
- give unsubstantiated opinions
2 Say what you think of the novel and why.
3 Analyse the meaning and effectiveness of the author's words.
4 Structure.
5 AO4.

Notes

PHILIP ALLAN
UPDATES

EVERYTHING YOU NEED FOR THE VERY BEST GRADES

Go to **www.philipallan.co.uk** to see our range of core texts and revision guides.